Playing Pygmalion

Playing Pygmalion

How People Create One Another

Ruthellen Josselson

JASON ARONSON
Lanham • Boulder • New York • Toronto • Plymouth, UK

Published in the United States of America
by Jason Aronson
An imprint of Rowman & Littlefield Publishers, Inc.

A wholly owned subsidiary of
The Rowman & Littlefield Publishing Group, Inc.
4501 Forbes Boulevard, Suite 200, Lanham, Maryland 20706
www.rowmanlittlefield.com

Estover Road
Plymouth PL6 7PY
United Kingdom

British Library Cataloguing in Publication Information Available

Library of Congress Cataloging-in-Publication Data

Josselson, Ruthellen.
  Playing Pygmalion : how people create one another / Ruthellen Josselson.
    p. cm.
  Includes bibliographical references.
  ISBN-13: 978-0-7657-0487-0 (cloth : alk. paper)
  ISBN-10: 0-7657-0487-0 (cloth : alk. paper)
  ISBN-13: 978-0-7657-0488-7 (pbk. : alk. paper)
  ISBN-10: 0-7657-0488-9 (pbk. : alk. paper)
  1. Expectation (Psychology). 2. Social perception. 3. Identity (Psychology)—
Social aspects. I. Title.

  BF323.E8J67 2007
  155.9'2—dc22   2007004381

Printed in the United States of America

∞™ The paper used in this publication meets the minimum requirements of
American National Standard for Information Sciences—Permanence of Paper
for Printed Library Materials, ANSI/NISO Z39.48-1992.

DEDICATION

To my mentors who, in my mind, have sculpted what I have become: Joseph B. Adelson, Margaret Rioch, and Irvin D. Yalom

The difference between a flower girl and a lady is not how she behaves, but how she's treated.

George Bernard Shaw, *Pygmalion*

Contents

Foreword

"Did I find you or did I create you?" This is one of the fundamental questions of relationships, echoing an insight of the psychoanalyst D. W. Winnicott. But it is a question that is seldom asked either aloud or privately. All relationships involve both finding and creating. Other people have characteristics that have evolved from their unique relational histories and we are drawn to them on the basis of these characteristics. Yet which characteristics we see in others, which we amplify in them, and which we manage to implant in them—these are all the work of creation.

The unconscious streams of ourselves flow together in our intimate relationships. While it may often seem to people—and to the helping professionals who work with them—that others in their lives are *found*, that they exist in an already-formed state, just as often as they are created. These acts of creation occur unconsciously as the needs of the self take root in the hospitable soil of others' psyches and it is this coincidence of wish and fulfillment that bonds people together. The nature of the importance of others resides in the specific needs that seek expression and often these needs are at odds with what is consciously experienced or wished for. Thus, people can need intimate others to embody the shadow sides of themselves or to be a punishing force, all the while proclaiming their rage for or hatred of this "bad" other—and being locked in relationship with him or her.

Relationships are made rather than found. Psychoanalytic theory offers a wealth of understanding of how people unconsciously create what they both need and dread. But these processes are not well understood by most therapists. Too often, therapists join their patients in overlooking their own role in creating the relationships in their lives, such that it seems that patients were simply unfortunate to "have" an ungiving mother or to "find" an unloving spouse. Because processes of creation in relationship are largely unconscious, they are much harder to see. As a result, most theorists of relationships acknowledge that these processes exist but offer little language or explication for how they unfold or manifest themselves. This book is an effort to trace in psychological terms the subtle interplay by which people create the other.

This book had three wellsprings. One was my fascination with the Rashomon-like qualities of the relational interviews I have been doing for many years. Relational stories told from two sides illuminate the fluid space *between* people where relationships are dynamically created and re-created. The second was my interest in bringing the concepts of transitional object experience and projective identification out of the consulting room and considering their operation in ordinary human experience. These have been well understood in the psychoanalytic situation and, increasingly, in the early phases of infant development, but not in terms of relationships in general. Thus, I take a developmental view of the evolution of mutually constitutive interweaving worlds (Stolorow et al., 2001). The third was my growing impatience at clinical case conferences (and in response to published case reports) with unexamined objectivism—when therapists describe the people in their patients' lives in terms of certainty—such as, "the patient *had* a narcissistic and demanding mother, or the patient's father *was* self-absorbed and controlling." "You mean, the patient *experienced* her mother as narcissistic and demanding or *felt that* her father was self-absorbed and controlling," I always grouchily correct. It is all too easy for psychologists and therapists to fall prey to the objectivist fallacy—that they can take at face value the descriptions people provide of others in their lives. (This is increasingly occurring in narrative research as well.) Keeping in mind the complexities of the creation of the intersubjective space is the much greater challenge. It is to encourage others to enlarge their awareness of these complexities that I set out to detail the processes by which we create the others in our lives.

Acknowledgments

O nly by examining real lives in progress can the understanding of human experience advance, but this is not without cost to those whose lives are subject to analysis. I am deeply grateful to the women and men, anonymous and well disguised in this work, who courageously shared their life histories with me and gave me permission to present them.

I wish to thank the Institute for Advanced Study at the Hebrew University of Jerusalem for a fellowship during which I drafted much of this book. The members of the A. K. Rice Institute, past and present, through group relations work, have provided opportunities for me to learn profoundly about how people create one another, and I am indebted to them. They are too numerous to name, but special thanks are due to Nancy Adams, Zachary Green, Tom Large, and Shelley Ostroff—and to three who influenced me deeply but died before I could learn all I might have from them: Faith Gabelnick, Marvin Skolnick, and LeRoy Wells.

I extend my gratitude to those who read various drafts of this work and provided thoughtful and useful comments: Judith Armstrong, Barbara Baumgartner, Evelyn Beck, Laura Feldbaum, Adrienne Berenson Goldberg, Susan Goldberg, Devon Jersild, Doug Kent, Amia Lieblich, Jim Marcia, Beverly Palmer, Debbie Richardson, Ines Roe, Pam Sheff, and Irvin Yalom. Special thanks to Beverly Palmer for her unflagging belief in this project and to my editor, Art Pomponio, for his support. I am enormously grateful to Jaimie Baron who is as wonderful a reader and editor for me as she is a daughter. I also thank my husband, Hanoch Flum, simply for being.

1

Creating One Another

INTRODUCTION

A year after Bob left their twenty-five-year marriage, Alice, a successful writer and editor, learned that he had taken up with Peggy, a somewhat younger, athletic businesswoman. Her friend reported to her that Bob and Peggy had just come back from St. Thomas, that Bob had become a serious wine expert and had taken up jogging and tennis. Alice was dumbfounded. "Bob always hated going to the beach—I never could get him to spend more than a day at anything like a resort. And he despised exercise and people who exercised, always making jokes about them. And as to wine—he felt the same way about anything alcoholic as he did about exercise and beaches. I can't believe it's the same person."

This is hardly an uncommon experience. Someone you think you know embarks on a new relationship and seems to transform overnight. Love seems to recreate them, and we might, like Alice, feel that we never really knew this person, even someone with whom we lived for twenty-five years.

How can we explain such happenings? Were we blind to aspects of the person that were there all along? Do people just transform when they change partners? Do people "bring out" aspects of others that are beyond someone else's reach? After all, liking the beach, exercise, and wine seem like "givens" of personality, not tastes that can be changed at will, especially not in midlife.

There have, of course, been many ways to explain the endless complexity of life with others, in literature, philosophy, psychology, and sociology. No one framework could possibly contain all the various ways of understanding the infinite forms of engagement and misunderstanding we have with one another. Systems theories in psychology and sociology have looked at relational life as a form of interlocking patterns that people create that sustain them in particular ways of being toward each others, patterns that, once established, are very difficult to change.

In this book, I am interested in analyzing the ways in which people "create" one another through unconscious psychological activity. Rather than regarding people as having indelible characters, I think of people as mutable characters with the potentiality to be enlisted into each other's ongoing scripts. Each of us is like a theater director, casting others into roles on our stage, even as others are casting us into their dramas.

In some plays, scripted for similarity, one person may take on and enjoy what a person they are close to enjoys. In other plays, scripted for difference, the fact that one person likes something will lead the other to dislike it. Change the scene or the cast of characters and the props and dialogues of life may change as well.

Our effects on one another's being, however, go much deeper and are far broader than likes and dislikes. Psychologists have long understood psychoanalysis to be a theater on whose stage our psychic repertoires are enacted.[1] In a psychoanalytic therapy, the patient will eventually "create" in the therapist the characters who have become part of his or her psychic life, and psychoanalysis has been dedicated to understanding how these scenarios play out in the analytic situation, how the analyst is recruited into various roles in the inner life of the patient.[2] But these processes are not limited to the psychotherapeutic situation. In the course of life, we all to some extent are in the role of the analyst, buffeted by the pressure to live out aspects of the psyche of those with whom we are in close contact. And we similarly "create" the others with whom we live interdependently. Mind itself, says psychoanalyst Stephen Mitchell (1988), is a composite of relational configurations. The psychotherapeutic situation is unique only in that it takes these processes as an object of study. In life, we simply live them out, seldom aware of our own role in creating the others who live on our own private stage or the roles we enact for others in their interior dramas.

We create ourselves and our relationships in interaction with one another. We recruit people to be characters in dramas that we are enacting even as they recruit us to be characters in theirs. Seldom do we look too closely at who we are in others' lives as long as they are satisfactorily enacting the character we need in our own. When Howard, husband of one of my patients, Lynn, left her after five years, he told her, "You are not *you* anymore." She spent the next two years in therapy trying to understand what he could possibly have meant by this. Lynn had felt so uplifted, so valued by Howard's love, and they had had what she had felt was an extraordinarily intimate and fulfilling relationship. In the end, she had to live with the painful recognition that the Lynn he had constructed and loved was not the same as the person she believed she was and had always been. In effect, Howard could no longer find in her the creation he had made of her, and Lynn was left wondering if he had ever really loved *her.*

In *War and Peace,* Prince Andrey, emerging from a period of depression and hopelessness, falls in love with Natasha when he overhears her rhapsodizing out loud on her enchantment with the beauty of the night. To him, she embodies the spirit of joy and renewal and he falls in love with her without ever even having spoken to her. "Prince Andrey was conscious in Natasha of a special world, utterly remote from him, brimful of joys unknown to him, that strange world, which . . . had tantalised him. . . . He looked at Natasha singing, and something new and blissful stirred in his soul" (p. 435). This feeling lasts only until he asks her to marry him, after which "some sudden reaction seemed to have taken place in his soul; there was none of the poetic and mysterious charm of desire left in it; instead there was pity for her feminine and childish weakness, terror at her devotion and trustfulness" (p. 447). Natasha seems to magically transform into a sweet, weak, devoted child. Andrey is an intellectual, much older than she. Natasha is not sure what he wants of her. She wonders, "What is it he seeks in me? What is it he is probing for with that look? What if I haven't in me what he is searching for in that look?" (p. 440). Swept away by the thrill of his interest in her, Natasha, a romantic at heart, doesn't question too deeply. It suffices that he desires her, and she is determined to be whatever he wants her to be.

We are characters in each other's life stories. But the role that we are assigned and enact is seldom identical with the whole person we know ourselves to be. We follow a script determined by largely unconscious forces where parts of ourselves meld with what others, because of who they are, need us to be. Our meanings for them never encompass all that we are. And we enact what they need us to be because they are doing the same for us. In Pirandello's play, *Six Characters in Search of an Author*, the Director says, "I'm sorry to have to tell you that yours is not the only part. There are also the others. . . . You can't have a character invading the scene and becoming so dominant that he overpowers the others. All of them have to be contained in a harmonious framework and then act out what is actable. I too am well aware of the fact that everyone has his own interior life which he would like to bring out into the open. But the difficulty is precisely this: to bring out into the open only what is important in reference to the others" (p. 49). What is "actable" in our lives are only those scripts that we find others who are willing, however reluctantly, to share. Together we create the drama. Master and slave, lover and loved one, teacher and student. One cannot exist without the other.

Sometimes others may know parts of ourselves that we don't know, and part of their (unconsciously agreed-upon) role in our life may be protecting us from that knowledge. Those closest to us are most likely to know our faults and those who love us most are least likely to tell us about them. Rather, those who love us quietly make up for what we lack or cover our indiscretions. If this is done well, our faults may seem to us to disappear. Thus, who we "are" for each other is a complex mixture of needs and desire on both sides. This is what makes relationships so exciting, so necessary, and, often, so difficult.

Every relationship "feels" different from every other one. The emotional cadences of each relationship have their own rhythm and melody, not duplicated exactly anywhere else. Being with one friend evokes in us subtle differences in emotional experience and self-expression unique to that relationship, distinct from being with any other friend. With one friend, we are more ready to laugh at other people's foibles, with another, we resonate together with intellectual ironies. The way we speak together is unique: with one, we are more ready to use salty language; with another, we bring our highest form of discourse. This is not just a matter of different shared interests. It has more to do with the coming together of different parts of ourselves with carefully selected parts of others.

Relationships are not expressible in language. They are *felt* more than thought. We can talk about them but never fully reproduce them in words. While great authors are adept at painting with words the interior spaces of relationships, we nevertheless, if we stand back, have to recognize that no one we know really talks that way. Scenes don't end when crucial revelations are made. We still have to go about the daily business of being together in which the emotional dynamics of the relationship are carried implicitly, on undercurrents that reside beneath the surface of what we actually say to one another. Whether we pay attention to it or not, we are always "reading" our meaning for the other and constructing their meaning to us.

What we are "reading" is emotional tone—and this goes beyond behavior and events. In fact, the same behavior changes radically if the emotional coloring is different. Martha and Fred returned home from work in a raging thunderstorm to discover that neither of them had shopped for dinner, each expecting the other to have done so. While ordinarily, in their relational system, this would have been an occasion for a bout of blaming each other and sulking, they instead, because they were feeling good about the other person, turned this occasion into a peanut butter and jelly picnic. Because neither wanted to go out in the rain again and because they were too hungry to wait for a pizza delivery, peanut butter and jelly was the only viable solution. But they could have eaten their simple sandwiches either playfully or angrily—and this is what made all the difference to their sense of themselves and each other.

The primary thing that happens in relationships is that we induce emotional states in one another.[3] We say we like someone (or dislike them) based on how the other person "makes us feel." "I feel good being with him/her," we might say, or, "I don't know, just being with him/her gives me the creeps." But if we were to ask these speakers to be more definite about what they mean, they would likely be at a loss for words. Or, if they are more persistent at being articulate, they might point to a particular characteristic of the person in question to try to anchor their emotional experience. "She is always smiling," some might say to locate the source of the good feeling, or "There is something about the way he never looks me in the eye that makes my skin crawl." But these "characteristics" are not the source of the feeling. There are many people who smile a lot who don't make us feel good and lots of people who don't look us in the eye whom we find charming and enjoyable to be with. No, there is something more.

Relationship to others precedes language and even thought. From our earliest experiences as infants, we take in the peopled world around us through more primitive forms of knowing. We catch the waves of the anxiety or sadness in those around us. We feel their excitement and arousal, their attentiveness to us, and their joy and displeasure. By the time we learn to express ourselves in words and name our emotions, we have already had innumerable experiences knowing the relational world through our senses. Sometimes this has been called intuition, or empathy.

What we read in others, though, is never a simple measure of their affective experience. Rather, it is some melange of their feeling state and our own. Imagine a baby awakening feeling contented and alert. Mother enters the room tired and frustrated from a long day of work. Within a few seconds, a complicated transaction occurs. Either the baby will catch a whiff of mother's tension and low mood and become fussy and anxious— or mother will be energized by her baby's high spirits and they will begin to coo at one another. Whichever way this plays out, one of them will have induced the other with their own emotional state.

Relating to others always involves such shared negotiation of emotional states. When I see my friend Irene, I feel prepared to be enlivened and excited, to talk about things that matter to me with someone who, I know, shares a lot of my reactions, and I think this is how Irene feels on seeing me. If Irene happens to be in a low mood, I will try to restore her to the person I expect her to be. "You are not yourself today," I might say. But of course she is. She is just a different part of herself than I am accustomed to. Still, my expectation of how we are together is very likely to distract her from whatever is troubling her and we will find a way to chatter together in our usual way. And Irene is then likely to experience me as having cheered her up.

With Jim, however, whom I have known for thirty-five years, I don't usually feel stimulated or excited, but I value his calm presence and a belief that he will always be available and responsive to me. With him, I feel a security and acceptance that I treasure. But I find myself telling him lots of stories since I know at some level that he looks to me for amusement and entertainment; he is intrigued by my emotional displays and confusion, my daring and irreverence, so much in contrast to his steadiness and predictability. Jim thinks of me (I think) as his eccentric, interesting friend and indeed with him, I feel free to express my more irrational and ambivalent sides, knowing that whatever I say or do, he will absorb it without judgment or advice.

People's sense of reality is constructed in interconnection with those who make up their social world. There is not an "out there" world to be perceived accurately or inaccurately.[4] Instead, we together create a reality that we live in. Thus, when we have in mind certain "characters" that we need in our world and find people who seem to live out those characteristics, and who find in us characters that fit into the reality they aim to construct, then we together shape a script or play that we will live in together. Seldom do we investigate too closely whether these people who are important to us are in some sense "really" what they seem to be for us. We regard others as being somehow just already *there* in the outside world.

We assign people to parts and then unconsciously induce them to engage us in enacting the complementary part. People can seem to have an almost magical transformative positive influence on us—when we are ready to change for the better. The climactic line in the popular movie, *As Good As It Gets*, is when Jack Nicholson tells Helen Hunt, "You make me want to be a better man." This line is moving because we all recognize the way in which others may draw from us our own best selves. But it also speaks to how our experiences of ourselves and our lives are engendered by our interconnections with others. We find in others wellsprings for our own goals and motivations, although we cannot articulate just what in this other person does this to us. Are we creating them as muses or is it something in them that impels us? This is perhaps one of the most important, but unanswerable, questions of human life.

Relationships are created between people through delicate unconscious negotiations about feeling states and aspects of self that do or do not have a place in the script. Independently, however, we create an image of who the other person "is" and what they mean to us. And this is a convincing portrait. As a third party, listening to someone tell us about someone who is important in their life, we, too, come to feel that we "know" that person. What we know is who that person is to the teller. If and when we actually meet that person, however, we are likely to feel confused, because that person doesn't seem to match up with how we have come to "know" them so far—through our friend's account.

Again and again, in clinical work, I have felt that I have come to "know" someone's mother through the detailed accounts of my patient. I build, for example, a picture of a domineering, intrusive, critical woman who has no understanding of her daughter and, with my patient, feel angry at her. Then, when I have had the opportunity to actually meet this witch-mother, I invariably find someone very different from what I had conjured. I find that, from the mother's perspective, her attempts at empathy have been rebuffed, that she feels that "nothing I ever say is right no matter how hard I try," that she feels at a loss for how to connect with a daughter who seems to be dismissing her at every turn. I learn over and over that people are not identical with how others experience them.

The characters we create in our lives are not all helpful or benign. We are equally likely to embody our inner demons in others. The critical, persecuting part of ourselves is likely to be spoken by someone close to us, in part because it is easier to do battle with what is external to us than with what resides inside us. Or the self-absorbed mother we learned to humor in childhood seems to live on in a partner or close friend, providing us the double-edged security of painful familiarity.

Lily, for example, went out of her way to keep the house "perfect" for her husband, changing the sheets each day, warming his dinner plate, worrying that something might displease him. Her father had seemed consistently critical of her—and to look at Lily, whose understated makeup was always beautifully applied, whose fashionable clothes were always exquisitely matched and pressed, one could see how high were her standards for herself. But whether she found a demanding husband or created him this way is an open question. Ken insisted that he didn't care that the house was so perfect even though he felt pampered and pleased by Lily's careful touches. Still, it is not just a simple matter of saying that Lily was deluded. Rather, there was a complicated system between them in which Lily needed a demanding man to please, but Ken needed a doting woman whose attentions he could claim not to need.

We stage our private dramas through unconscious processes that cast the characters with uncanny accuracy. The basis on which we consciously think we are casting is usually deceptive and camouflages the deeper, unconscious foundation for the choice. Danielle and Roger seemed to be perfect for one another—both attractive, brilliant, successful, and eager to engage in a relationship and create a family together. They were in love and thought they had found the perfect partner. Danielle said she had never found such a kind, empathic, warm, and loving man. Roger felt enchanted with Danielle's intelligence and sense of humor as well as her responsiveness to him, the way she seemed to really understand him. But two years later, Danielle found herself living with her abusive father, now enacted by Roger, and Roger found himself shielding himself from his unpredictable, irrational mother who Danielle became for him. Both felt completely misunderstood by the other. In complex and subtle ways, each drove the other to be exactly what each most wanted to escape from. Each had unconsciously recognized in the other the hidden capacity to enact his or her own worst fear and then, also unconsciously, set about drawing that capacity into the drama. Regardless of who Roger may be to himself, or who Danielle may be to herself, they make each other heroes or villains—and that makes all the difference in how both their lives unfold.

Over many years of living with other people, seeing patients individually and in groups, and trying to help them live with other people, I have been occupied with the question of who we are for one another. In my research on relationships, I ask people to draw maps of their significant relationships over time and to narrate the ways in which these people have been important to them. When I have interviewed people who appear on each other's maps, I have been astonished by the ways in which the role that one person plays in the other's life is so dramatically different from the meanings the other assigns to him or her. In this book, I intend to tell some of these stories and analyze the dynamic nuances of relational co-construction by focusing on two important processes: creating illusions and creating the other.

THE CREATION OF ILLUSION

The psychoanalyst D. W. Winnicott revolutionized psychological understanding with his important concepts of transitional phenomena marking the intermediate area of experience that he calls illusion (1975). This space of illusion is an amalgam of inner and outer reality, lying between what is subjective and what is objectively perceived. Winnicott wondered at the psychological significance to the baby of the cherished blanket or teddy bear. His insight was that this object stood for the absent good mother and could be a comfort in her absence. Most important, though, is that the teddy bear just *is* a comfort, without the child having to ask whether or not the comfort comes from the bear or from the emotional investment he or she has made in the bear. In other words, the child doesn't ask him or herself, "Did I find this or did I create it?" This space of illusion—the capacity to invest physical objects or other people with qualities that derive from our own inner world—persists throughout life. In an area between me and not-me, between fantasy and reality, this space of illusion contains the tension between what is internal and what is external (Ogden, 1992).

To look too closely at such an illusion—at any age—is a form of skepticism, an overuse of reality testing that would make our world sterile and cold.

Illusion is different from delusion or hallucination, both of which derive solely from the inner world. While a delusion is real to the person who experiences it, it has no basis in shared reality. Illusion, however, is an interpretation of something that exists, an investment of meaning in something perceived. The person or thing that comforts exists, but it is we ourselves who endow it with its meaning and make comfort possible. This process of endowing something with meaning marks the critically important space between imagination and external reality, a space where reality appears to us as being what it is without our having to investigate whether it is simply "there" or whether we have had a part in creating its meaning for us. Play is another example of transitional experience, a realm in which we can pretend in a real way. Thus, the child can make a tower that both is and is not real. Art and cultural symbols are more mature forms of this fundamental duality, being both things in themselves and creations of our own. A religious monument is "just" a building but is also a holy place, and we treat its holiness as residing in its essence even though we also know our own role in creating it as a place of transcendent meaning. These transitional phenomena mediate between our inner worlds of psychic reality and the outside world of consensual reality, and what matters most is that we do not attend to the origins of what we experience.[5] If we were to do so, the teddy bear would become, to the baby, the "dirty smelly old thing" it is to his mother, and Jerusalem would become just one of many cities of the world.

We are most familiar with illusion in states of falling in love. Shakespeare, well aware of this, enshrined it in *A Midsummer Night's Dream*, making a comedy out of people's tendency to idealize the beloved. Illusion is clearest in others, of course. I recall a weekend in Paris many years ago, spent with John, a man who was in love—not with me, but with Michelle, a close friend of mine. I, too, had fallen in love that week—with Eduoard. Both the objects of our passion had left the city and, finding ourselves each on our own, we kept each other company as we enjoyed Paris. Together we reveled in the exquisite sensation of being in love and extolled to each other the exceptional virtues of our respective "amours." The Michelle I knew, of course, had little to do with the Michelle John thought *he* knew. Therefore, his processes of illusion were clear to me. While I was quite able to restrain myself from the absurdity of challenging his ideas about her, I was equally unable to recognize that I, too, was constructing for myself an Eduoard who, in reality, had little relation to my own imagination of him. To me, during that time, Eduoard simply *was* the beautiful, brilliant, enchanting French man I thought I had encountered.

In the end, neither of these relationships survived the blasts of reality that later experience provided, but John and I remained friends for quite a long time, a friendship based on having deeply shared the processes of illusion.

Illusions may seem like reality itself, even over long periods of time, often until there is a painful, rude awakening and the person (rather than the relationship) seems to transform into someone completely different. Catherine, a middle-aged woman, awakening from her own love dream, told me,

> When I saw Matt again, a year later, I could no longer even imagine what I saw in him. He had been a friend and had seemed to me the handsomest, smartest, funniest, person I had ever known and we really had something special between us. Four years of building an illusion, one year of thinking of nothing but him after I fell hard in love with him, until he made it clear that he did not want that kind of relationship with me—and what emerged from behind the curtain was a dull, superficial, stoop-shouldered, somewhat childish man. His efforts to joke now seemed vapid rather than clever, his conversation hackneyed. I realized that all of what had seemed lively and exciting between us had been coming from me. When I turned down the volume, the music died. And yet I am still filled with longing for what I felt the one night we made love. The wish fulfilled. Holding in my arms everything I ever wanted in a man—stroking him, feeling him respond to my touch. After he left that night, I said to myself, Now I can die happy. I stayed up all night then, afraid that if I slept, I wouldn't be sure if it had just been a dream. And now, of course, I know that it happened, but it was also just a dream. When I think back on it now, clear-sighted, I'm not at all sure he was feeling what I was feeling or even what I thought he was feeling. I filled in for him. I felt I could "know" what he felt without his having to put his feelings into words. I still think I may have felt some passion from him—but who knows—was it his—or mine?

Besides idealizing illusions in states of being in love, we can form all sorts of illusions about people, depending on what we need. We imagine that others are what we wish (or fear) them to be and may overlook or dismiss behavior or cues from them that don't fit our script. We are always engaged in inferring others' internal states and responses to us and these often have the character of Winnicott's transitional phenomena—is it there or did I imagine it?[6]

Because we can never directly observe another person's inner state, our understanding of what goes on in others is always a result of our interpretations of them. And our understandings of others are always mapped onto how we understand our own inner experience, which is the only inner experience we can know directly. Early in life we come to know ourselves as beings constituted by thoughts and feelings that emanate from inside us. As infants, these inner experiences are interpreted for us by others who teach us that a certain bodily, emotional experience is called "anger" or "sadness." Gradually, we also come to learn that others have inner states, different from ours, and as we grow up even more, we develop ideas about how their inner states connect to their behavior—and to ours. "We can't eat these cookies that mother just baked," says Dick, a child of eight, to his younger sisters, Maggie and Jill, "or mother will get angry." "No, she won't get angry if we're good and eat just a few, " says Maggie. "Who cares if she's angry?" says Jill. Here we have three siblings constructing very differently the potential emotional state of their mother. Dick has understood and experienced the possibility of his mother's anger to mean he must desist from eating the cookies, however tempting they may be. For him, his mother's anger is very powerful and frightening. Maggie has in her mind a different model of what does and does not evoke mother's anger or feels confident in her ability to mollify her. Jill regards her mother's anger as irrelevant to herself and her own behavior. All of them, then, are constructing, to a large extent, a different mother, or, to be more precise, a different self in relation to mother and mother in relation to self. These three children have the same physical mother, but three different illusory mothers, and it is the illusory mothers that will be most important in their own development. We can witness the seeds of what may later in their lives become their interpersonal styles, determined by the scripts they tend to live out—and enlist others to live out with them. We may see here an early version of what later becomes Dick's subservience (and his need to find someone to obey), Maggie's charm (and her ability to find others who will allow her to charm them out of their own wishes), or Jill's rebelliousness against authorities (whom she enlists to try to constrain her).

These illusions may also be very powerful in affecting their mother's behavior as well. Sensing Dick's fear of her anger, she may be likely to be more gentle with him, although Dick would be unlikely to experience her this way if his illusion is well-formed. With Maggie, mother may allow herself to be sweet-talked and charmed, especially if she sees in Maggie some of her own (cherished) tendencies to get her own way through seductiveness. But Jill's disregard of her feelings is likely to evoke harsh treatment from her mother, if only to feel that she exists and has an impact, as she feels a mother should. There is a circular process between illusion and creation of the other. We both become and react against what others have made of us even as they become and react against what we have made of them.

Illusion, then, is the sum of the qualities that we endow something with. If something is completely external to us, then it is perceived, but we have no felt relationship to it. There are many human beings whom we perceive, but unless we have some sense of investing them with something of ourselves, of making them part of our emotional experience, then they are just beings in the world, not in *our* world.

There is an enormous range of possibility within illusionary processes, depending in part on how near to us other people are. We create others whom we experience at a distance differently from those who are very close to us, but the process of such creation, the interplay of what is internal and what is external, remains similar.

Through the process of illusion formation, for example, we can create a sense of felt relationship to someone just barely known. Recently, I was sitting with a group of colleagues and the talk moved to basketball. Someone mentioned Magic Johnson and his altruistic ways of teaching young players. One of my colleagues burst out, "I met him once" and related the circumstances of being in his presence and introduced to him, however briefly. It was clear from this discussion that for him Magic Johnson, now imbued with memory and a fleeting handshake, had a different meaning than he had for us. He had been uplifted by this brief experience and, in some strange way, empowered to be more charitable. For my colleague, an experience of illusion—or at least, a different sort of illusion—connected them. (Magic Johnson, for his part, tries to make use of these illusory processes to inspire young boys in positive ways.)

We create illusions of others to stand for idealized states of being and we also create others as denigrated people to represent what we despise most in ourselves. In our culture, we create illusions about celebrities to serve a variety of psychological needs in the society. The media obsessively glamorize the lives of the "rich and famous" to serve our collective need for the illusion that someone is living a life where every wish is satisfied. Equally obsessively, we need then to devalue such icons, to find their clay feet or personal tragedy in order to reassure ourselves that no one is living a life of such gratification. Often, we both need the illusion and need to destroy it. It is then both satisfying and shocking to learn that Marilyn Monroe spent lonely Saturday nights without a date—interrupting our illusion of her unassailable incarnation as an object of desire. And a friend of mine, who recently had the opportunity to interview Jane Fonda over breakfast, called me excitedly to report that Jane Fonda eats heartily! Similarly, our collective and irrational need for the illusion of moral perfection in our leaders (and our readiness to denigrate them) led to national horror when Americans were forced to confront the human aspects of a president who succumbed to sexual temptation.

People closer to hand are subject to similar illusionary processes. As we get to know people better, we have myriad opportunities for both perception and illusion. In a relationship with another person, we are bombarded with information about that person, how they look, sound, laugh, how they move through space, all the things they say, and all the nuances of feeling and response to us they express. Of these, we take in just a few aspects that capture our attention; we select, usually outside of our awareness, those bits of a person that are meaningful to us because of the sensitivities and proclivities that form our individual and unique psychic reality. We take in what seem to be a person's actual qualities and mix these perceptions with our own histories, needs, and expectations to form an image of who this person "is." Our view of them is, then, a product of these processes of illusion, although it may seem to us that we are experiencing reality as it is given to us rather than interpreting it. But if we stop and think about it, we recognize the importance of ourselves as the artist who is composing the picture.[7]

Annette and Shari were both new members of a church board. At the first meeting, David responded to another board member's suggestion by citing passages from Dostoevsky from memory. Annette instantly idolized him. Like a moth drawn to a flame, she was mesmerized by his brilliance and his knowledge and targeted him as someone she wanted to get closer to. Shari, on the other hand, found him arrogant and condescending and had doubts about whether she wanted to be part of the group at all. "I've never even *read* Dostoevsky," she said to Annette later. These two women, then, constructed in their minds very different Davids.

We create illusions by interpreting other people's behavior, putting a gloss of meaning on what they do by how we frame it to ourselves. We construct stories about the other, making sense of their behavior along the lines that we need to see them. Someone who firmly stands his or her ground without giving way can be seen as either willful and stubborn or full of integrity, depending on the light in which we wish to cast the behavior. Directness can be seen as rudeness or as authenticity, shyness as social awkwardness or as reserve. It all depends on how we "take in" and interpret another's qualities.

Without being fully aware of it, we are constantly interpreting others, although it seems to us that people simply are what we make of them and are "really" doing what we construe their actions to mean. The script we are creating controls how we interpret our interactions with others. For example: Gary's wife, Gina, is picking him up after a business meeting and arrives, half an hour late, with their three-month-old son, their first child, in the car. Excitedly and hurriedly, Gary calls his business associate and says, "Hey, come meet my baby." He pulls the baby from the car and proudly shows him off to the associate, then says good-bye and gets in the car. Gary doesn't introduce Gina, which Gina notices and Gary does not. Gina, if she is sensitized to rejection, concludes that Gary loves the baby more than her, since he didn't even acknowledge her existence to his colleague. Or Gina may assimilate this experience to an image of her husband as socially inept—he never did have any manners—and at least be happy that he was acting like a proud father. Or Gina may conclude that Gary is annoyed at her for being late or in a hurry to get to their dinner engagement; or that he had some good reason for not introducing her that he will tell her about. Or Gina may be so focused on getting to their dinner party in all that traffic and so uninterested in being part of Gary's work life that she doesn't make anything of it at all. Or Gina may feel so identified with their baby and share so deeply in Gary's excitement about him that she may feel she has, in effect, been included. The interpretation Gina puts on this interaction will both reflect and confirm the script that she feels herself to be enacting with Gary. If, for example, Gina is scripting rejection, then this scene "proves" that Gary is rejecting her. If she needs to regard Gary as socially inept (and herself as the socially able one), then this scene adds to her construction of him as not knowing how to behave with others unless she instructs him how to do so. Or perhaps her intolerance of his anger has forced Gary to express his anger in passive-aggressive ways. Then this incident would only confirm to Gina that Gary acts angrily without acknowledging it. There are many other possible interpretations Gina could have made—these are just a few. We can see, then, how interpreting through our scripts offers us self-confirming evidence, and our "illusions" are maintained. Just about any incident can be melded to any pre-existing script, and if not, it can be ignored and forgotten.

In common parlance, we may dismiss a perception we had in the past by saying, "but it was just an illusion." In doing so, we mean that we now recognize that what seemed to us a perception was mainly a product of our imagination. But this is a way of disregarding the illusory processes that mark all relationships—as though *only* that particular perception was a product of illusion. "It was just an illusion" means it was an illusion I could no longer maintain in the face of experience, which required that I modify it or give up my capacity for reason and reality testing.

Listen to two women discussing a third, even having a trivial discussion. "I think Tammy is really nice," says one. "I don't. I think she's really full of herself and out for what she can get from people. I wouldn't trust her for a minute," says the other. If we are naïve realists, we might seek to discover whether or not Tammy is "really" nice or self-centered. If we are more psychologically informed, however, we would recognize that both people are responding to different aspects of Tammy and are responding in terms of their own inner worlds. Each will pick out incidents and observations of Tammy to support her point of view—and the two speakers will trade conflicting stories about her. But one will not persuade the other to change her opinion, since the reaction of each is rooted in her own idiosyncratic responsiveness to people by which she interprets her interpersonal reality. Perhaps the first speaker is habitually ready to see the good in others and is inclined to give them the benefit of the doubt. Perhaps the second has felt herself to have been betrayed in friendship and is sensitive to others' duplicity. Or perhaps it is her own struggles with self-centeredness that make her attuned to this in others. There is then no "reality" of Tammy beyond each person's construction, even though neither thinks about the role she herself is playing in that construction—and they will continue to argue (hopelessly) about how Tammy "is."

Usually we have some awareness of how others view us, although we may be somewhat mystified by why some people seem so consistently to misunderstand us. If we reflect on it, we can recognize some of the meanings we have for others, that is, what they are making of us in their own lives. Often, however, we may have profound effects in the lives of others who have little or no meaning in our own. Recently I met a (barely remembered) former student who told me earnestly that something I had said years ago changed her life and that she thinks of me each day. I have no memory of saying what she remembers. Any teacher has such a story. Perhaps all people do, although they may not learn about the influence they have wielded in another's life. We utter something, or represent something, at a crucial moment when someone was poised to change and we come to be enshrined as the catalyst of such change.

CREATING THE OTHER

Beyond creating private illusions of the other through our interpetations of them, we can also, through powerful unconscious processes, evoke in others aspects of ourselves or others from our past. When these processes are operating, the illusion goes beyond our own minds and actually creates change in the other person. We induce them to play the parts we want, need, or expect them to play—even if this wasn't their predilection. This phenomenon is best known from psychotherapy, but it occurs in all human relationships. The therapist, for example, may find herself feeling critical of her patient, even though she is trained and well able to maintain a nonjudgmental stance. With therapeutic work, both therapist and patient come to understand that the critical judgment she feels derives from a projection into her of the patient's critical father. The patient has, through unconscious means, implanted in the therapist the reproving person that he is struggling to contend with in his own inner world. Conflict is always easiest to deal with externally. So if we can take what is internally troubling and create it outside ourselves, it is still problematic, but less painful than if the negative experience is felt as part of our inner world. Thus, for the patient, the formula is something like, "It is not that

I hate myself for being imperfect, as my father hated me for being imperfect, it is you who are hating me for my failures and I will see to it that you really feel this way about me in hopes that somehow it will all turn out differently." This can be true of any feeling state. I have often, with patients, had moments of feeling intense sadness, being on the verge of tears, while they are calm and collected but talking about something painful. Their sadness has been transported into me to manage for them.

These processes, termed *projective identification* in psychoanalytic writings, can sometimes sound magical or mystical, but, with careful analysis, one can see them as ubiquitous unconscious processes that mark all human relationships.[8] Freud (1915) himself was astonished at the range of unconscious communication and noted, "It is a very remarkable thing that the unconscious of one human can react upon the other without passing through consciousness" (p. 194).

Object relations theory has created our understanding that in important relationships of grown-up life, people "find" others who psychologically resemble their parents of childhood and treat them in the same ways. The concept of projective identification, however, goes beyond this in attending to how people actually induce in others the emotional states that recreate early experiences.[9] In that sense, through unconscious communication, needed others are created rather than simply found. (Still, like all good directors, we are attentive to casting as well as script and must find suitable candidates for the roles we unconsciously wish to assign.)

In a close relationship, in which we are open to emotional exchange with another person, we resonate with the unconscious feelings of that person, creating an unconscious conversation in which we negotiate emotional complementarity. We may use others as parts of ourselves, for example, unconsciously encouraging them to express feelings we find unacceptable in ourselves and then punishing them for it. At other times, we may succeed in (unconsciously) cajoling others to enact what we need. Catherine, for example, might have succeeded in getting Matt to try to "become" her ideal man—depending on his unconscious needs.

In groups, certain people are unconsciously "chosen" by the group to embody certain aspects—rebellion, rescue, anger, incompetence, wisdom, and so on. Once certain others have been so elected, everyone else can feel free of these aspects of themselves. How often, for example, have each of us had the experience of sitting silently in a group while someone else goes out on a limb and expresses the dissatisfaction that we were afraid to voice? The "complainer," however, may be unaware of having been "chosen" to speak for us.

Who we are is in part constructed out of those qualities others have tagged us with or induced in us. We all have certain characteristics that increase the likelihood that we will be regarded in particular ways or chosen to enact certain roles with particular others or in specific situations.[10] In psychological language, this is called having a *valence* to be recruited for a particular role. But we may carry many valences that can be called forth as the dynamics of the situation demand. Anyone who is a member simultaneously of a number of groups is well aware of this—in one group, one is a leader, in another, a rebel, in yet a third, a relatively peripheral member to whom few people pay much attention. And yet, one has the sense of being the same person and offering the same kind of input in each situation. But in one group, one's ideas are followed, which creates oneself as a leader; in the second group, one's ideas are regarded as rebellious and outrageous (and therefore one is likely to behave in more rebellious and outrageous ways); while in the third, no one is very interested in what one suggests. The same person can be a hero or a fool, depending on the interpersonal context.

As a culture, we have recently begun to be cognizant of the ways in which women have been "elected" to carry emotional experience for men. Socially inhibited from emotional expression, it is not uncommon for men to live their own feelings through a woman or women that they are close to. This is one of many examples of how projective identification can operate.

Scapegoats are people chosen to carry the bad qualities of others. In ancient Jewish tradition, a goat was chosen, everyone in the community transferred their sins to the goat, and the goat was ceremonially driven out, thus absorbing and eliminating the whole community's sins. Shirley Jackson, in her classic short story, "The Lottery," updates this legend in the tale of a community that yearly elects one person to be sacrified. Communities need scapegoats so that everyone else can remain unblemished—and not just someone to be sacrificed, but someone to actually enact whatever must be disowned. Adolescent girls are keenly aware of these processes as they form cliques based on excluding certain devalued other girls who then "become" the socially inept untouchables they have been singled out to be. All the other girls can then feel secure that they, at least, are untainted.[11] It has become a truism that what we most hate in others is what we cannot bear in ourselves. What is less apparent are the ways we actually "locate" these unbearable aspects of ourselves outside of ourselves.

We also may place into someone else all the wonderful characteristics we are not ready to acknowledge in ourselves or wish someday to have for ourselves. Such characters in our lives may appear to be ideal, perfect others whom we cherish because being with them engenders feelings of completion and satisfaction as though we were our own best, even perfect, selves. Others may live out for us the experiences we long for but fear. In this way, unavailable but precious aspects of ourselves are stored but not lost. At other times, people may be chosen because they exemplify parts of ourselves we feel unable to express, parts of ourselves that may have been lost or stunted because of our earlier experiences. If Wendy, who is shy, chooses Robin, who is outgoing and lively, for a best friend, then she remains in relation to a part of herself that she has split off and otherwise lost. In effect, then, Robin expresses for Wendy the exuberant, uninhibited part of Wendy. And Wendy is undoubtedly playing out some important function for Robin or they would not remain best friends. Perhaps Wendy is the admiring audience Robin needs.

At the most benign and mundane level, we may induce in others aspects of ourselves in order to feel a sense of similarity or closeness to them, promoting a sense of intimacy or sameness, making what was different or foreign feel familiar.[12] The other, then, may be unaware of whether this new aspect of self was there all along or somehow magically appeared, which in part explains what may have happened to Bob (with whom this chapter began) who, after leaving Alice and falling in love with Peggy, finds himself expressing himself in completely new ways. Depending on how he has constructed Peggy, this may lead him to enduring personal change or to backlash against what could come to feel like too much closeness and threatened merger.

When these processes are operating, a person is both the director and the principal actor in the drama. The other person becomes an unwitting actor in our drama to whom we subtly and unconsciously give stage directions (in return for enacting, in one way or another, their scripts). Sometimes these unconscious and crucial stage directions can be directly contradictory to what we say—in words and out loud—that we want the other person to do or be. For example, a woman can tell her husband that she wants him to be sensitive and empathic toward her, but then only respond to him sexually when he acts brutish and dictatorial. She is thus constructing him, projectively, as the "macho" man while insisting that she abhors this in him.

Sometimes we arrange for another person to feel what we find too painful to feel. We can, for example, induce others to worry for us. As I was writing this book, I was also involved in planning a major professional conference with a close friend and colleague. As the date of the conference drew nearer, she became very anxious about a plethora of details and I was the one who was always calm and reassuring—somewhat to my surprise since I am generally prone to worry. It was quite astonishing that, having satisfied herself that everything was under control just a few days before the conference, my friend stopped worrying—and I was quite unable to sleep that night because of anxiety about the conference. Once she had stopped "owning" the worry, it came flooding into me.

There are many instances where, through these processes, ambivalence is split between people and can shift in what can seem to be confusing ways. A couple I was seeing in therapy were looking for a house. They found one that the wife very much liked and wanted to buy, but her husband had a long list of doubts and reservations about it. Eventually, she gave up lobbying for this house and said that really she didn't like it that much after all, whereupon he decided that, all in all, this was the house he wanted.

We can, from the outside, see these processes of creating the other most clearly when we can witness people disowning aspects of themselves that are too painful to bear. In a recent consultation to an organization, for example, we were able to discern how the CEO, a dynamic, definitive sort of leader, sloughed off all fears of his own inadequacy by inducing everyone around him to feel inadequate and to hesitate to take any initiative. He was left fulminating: "How come I am the only one who can ever get anything done around here?" Although he was very distressed about feeling so unsupported by his staff, he was quite unaware of his own role in disempowering them. He was injecting feelings of inadequacy in his subordinates in all the usual ways: authorizing them to do tasks and undercutting them, micromanaging, giving them pep talks about simple jobs, and being displeased with any ideas that he hadn't thought of first. But he was doing all these things subtly, and if the organizational consultants concentrated on changing his behavior, the dynamics would just express themselves elsewhere. The core issue was his need to disown any sense of incompetence in himself, and it was this that was de-skilling those who worked for him. Once he could, through therapeutic intervention, accept his own fallibility and his need to depend on others for help, magically, it seemed to him, he discovered that he had some competent people around him.

I do not claim that *all* the qualities and behaviors we find in others are a result of our construction of them. But when processes of projective identification are in play, we have a stake in people being what they are for us and we are very resistant to their changing. We need them to be what they are for us, even if this way of being makes us frustrated, envious, or angry. Marital therapists witness again and again one partner refusing, usually subtly, to allow the other to change, even if it's in the direction they consciously wish him or her to be different.

We rarely consciously volunteer to play in others' dramas. Only with hindsight and much insight are we sometimes able to see that we have been playing a role in someone else's enactment of an aspect of his or her inner world.[13]

When these processes are operating, a kind of collusion exists between the players not to notice what is going on. For example, if a man arranges for his wife to treat him as his mother did, they will simply enact this scenario with neither of them able to take distance from it or put it into words. Because this drama is not intentionally or verbally scripted, it is very difficult to reflect on.[14] It is an enactment of something between the players, each taking part because of their own unconscious needs, and it eludes ready description in words. Through minute interactions and responses, through appeals and forms of coercion, both apparent and concealed, people negotiate who they will "be" for one another. The script, once carefully constructed, unfolds automatically.[15] It feels like "just how we are together."

When we unconsciously need people to be a certain way, when their being this way anchors our own psychological structure, then we are also rooted in seeing them in this way only and not in other ways. Thus, the woman who believes her husband to be stingy and withholding simply doesn't notice, or else devalues, the ways in which he is giving. For her own reasons, she needs to see herself as the nurturing, loving one and he shores up her self-image to the extent she can contrast herself with his ungiving nature.

We know ourselves only in interaction with others, and we play a role in both finding and creating the others with whom we intimately live. Other people can seem to bring us alive to something in our world or, by a gesture, glance, or remark, shrivel the reality in which we live.[16] There are, for all of us, moments that we can remember where a comment from someone else changed our lives—for better or worse—shattering a nascent dream or opening a new path. But we were not the passive recipients of these forces. It was our construction of the other that gave them the power to change our construction of ourselves.

Just as healthy children are born with the potential to speak any language, they are also born with the potential to express an infinite number of traits, or characteristic modes of response. Their early experiences act to solidify certain of these dispositions and to inhibit others. As people grow, transformative experiences are ones that call out other possibilities of being or behaving; parts of the self that had lain fallow come into expression. Such transformative experiences often involve encounters with others who engender or empower other aspects of self to flourish. As people construct others as characters, they enable (or coerce) others to reconstruct themselves. The world of others is infinite and shapeless until we give it form. In that sense, we are like Pygmalion, who, in the myth, fell in love with his own ivory sculpture of Galatea, a sculpture the goddess Venus later brought to life. We, too, sculpt others out of our needs and desires. Unlike Pygmalion, however, we are also being sculpted—our Galateas have their own needs and desires, their own subjectivities, even if we may wish this were not so.

KNOWING THE OTHER

Biographers are well aware of (and sometimes stymied by) the operation of both the creation of illusion and the creation of the other when they go in search of knowing what someone was "really like." Interviewing the many people who have known this person, they find themselves with contradictory portraits, as though the subject of the biography had many personalities.

This is equally apparent in ordinary lives. Who one is for others is very different from who one is to oneself, and people may be largely unaware of the script they are enacting for others. People do not realize that they have recruited other people onto their psychic stage and assigned them fairly specific parts. Unconsciously, they are on the lookout for suitable players to carry out the roles of the inhabitants of their inner worlds. And suitable players are ones who find a complementary partner for their own inner dramas. A small sign from one to another can be enough for the players to recognize their cue.

When we meet a new person, we wonder what this person is "like." But this question is really a question about what we are likely to call forth from this person—interest and engagement or contempt and dismissal, for example. Entering into a relationship involves negotiating the way we will each be constructed in this relationship, and every interchange determines which of the various parts of ourselves we will express toward one another.

Again, Tolstoy was a genius at portraying these processes:

> Prince Andrey regarded the immense mass of men as contemptible and worthless creatures, and he had such a longing to find in some other man the living pattern of that perfection after which he strove himself, that he was ready to believe that in Speransky he had found this ideal of a perfectly rational and virtuous man. Had Speransky belonged to the same world as Prince Andrey, had he been of the same breeding and moral traditions, Bolkonsky [Andrey] would soon have detected the weak, human, unheroic sides of his character; but this logical turn of mind was strange to him and inspired him with the more respect from his not fully understanding it. Besides this, Speransky, either because he appreciated Prince Andrey's abilities or because he thought it as well to secure his adherence, showed off his calm impartial sagacity before Prince Andrey, and flattered him with that delicate flattery that goes hand in hand with conceit, and consists in a tacit assumption that one's companion and oneself are the only people capable of understanding all the folly of the rest of the world and the sagacity and profundity of their own ideas. (p. 401)

Here Tolstoy shows us Andrey's readiness to construct Speransky in a certain way, to embody an ideal he was eager to find realized in a living person. It was Speransky's strangeness, his difference from the people in Andrey's customary relational world, that made it possible for Andrey to create his illusion. Tolstoy also depicts the mutuality of this process by suggesting the kind of meaning that Andrey might have had for Speransky. The fantasy of a special twosome with privileged vision is a not uncommon basis of many relationships.

Once relationships are established, aspects of the person that do not fit the script of the other, because they receive no emotional investment, are often not even perceived. Therefore, how the people closest to us might describe us, read our motives, and understand our way of relating to them would, if we could hear their story of us, surprise, maybe even shock, us. We might recognize ourselves in some of the depiction, but other aspects would leave us with the eerie feeling of "Can that be me who is being described?"

We see the other person through our relationship with him or her. We see their behavior, but not their experience.[17] We can never fully see inside their experience (of us) any more than they could see inside our experience (of them). In that other person's relational life, we are one of many characters, and to understand his or her story, we would have to see the whole pattern of characters who make up that life. Our importance and meaning in that person's life is always in the context of others who have had similar or different meanings. We would have to witness the interior of their life as a whole to understand our own part in it.

Who people are to us and who we are to others gets defined in the context of others who are already on stage. Thus, if we have many friends whom we regard as warmly supportive of us, we may be less likely to encourage another person's potential responsiveness to us. Linda, for example, admired her colleague in work, Janet, and wished to be closer to her and to be her friend; but Janet already had many friends to share experiences with and felt somewhat burdened by Linda's attention. She came to see Linda as clingy and intrusive and tried to keep away from her. In response to Janet's distance, Linda redoubled her efforts to get close to Janet, bringing her gifts and funny poems, which in turn made Janet work harder to get away from her. Linda began to think of Janet as snobbish and standoffish, and eventually she stopped trying to curry favor with her. To hear these two women tell it, Linda "is" needy and dependent according to Janet, while Janet "is" cold and hostile according to Linda. Neither sees that they have induced in the other the very behaviors that they dislike and that this stemmed from Janet not having available the role in her script that Linda wanted to occupy.

Frequently, we see similar phenomena as people search for romantic partners. Emerging from a relationship with Vince, a man whom she thought of (or constructed as) domineering and unempathic, Ellen cre-

ated a new relationship with Terry, a man who seemed warm and nurturing toward her. Only after several years did she come to experience
that Terry, too, was domineering and unempathic. Since Ellen was contrasting Terry to Vince, he seemed milder and less interested in controlling her. But, with time, she either became aware of qualities in Terry that
she had not allowed herself initially to see or else unconsciously induced
in Terry the same behaviors she had thought she escaped from. (Ellen's
story, though, told in exasperation, is "how come all men are so domineering and unempathic?")

When we hear people's stories of their lives, we generally grant that the
people who have been characters in their lives simply "are" as they have
been presented in the story. This is a customary suspension of disbelief,
enforced in part by our having learned that to question other people's
characterization of important players in their lives is to invite their wrath.
It is only when we can hear multiple stories about the same characters
that we begin to witness the complex processes that have contributed to
creating these people as they seem to be.

Stories of experiences in relationships reveal the "culture" that people
create through the others they invite and keep in their world.[18] The various relational dramas we all enact form the larger theatrical bill that constitutes our world. Some people live in a "culture" composed of people to
lean on and support them; others live in a world of people who demand
too much of them and appreciate them too little. Still others live in a
world of companions to enjoy experiences with but not to know or be
known by too deeply. And some people live in relational cultures that
have many possibilities for the construction of characters.

The "other people" who constitute a relational life, of course, are
known only through the complex processes by which we experience and
construct them. By asking another person for the stories of their relational
lives, we can understand something of how they construct relationships—
what aspects of other people capture their attention and imagination,
what they seek from others, and what impels them to maintain relationships and what leads them to abandon them. In these stories, of course,
people often share more of their experience than they intend to and we
might be able to infer ways in which processes of their own imagination,
unbeknown to themselves, create the illusions of the relationships in
which they live.

For each one of us, our life history is entangled with the life histories of
others.[19] We live out intertwined dramas. In this book, I present four parallel stories—two identical twin sisters, a mother and a daughter, a father
and a daughter, and a recently separated husband and wife. These are relational life stories, life stories told through the history of important relationships. Each member of the pair has been a star player in the other's

life. How does one twin construct the other? How do parents pass on to their children what has been most troubling in their psychological world? How do people find and create the partner that they both deeply need and can't bear to live with? In the interplay of these relational stories, we can see before us the ways in which people create one another—and struggle to live with the results.

NOTES

1. See also McDougall (1985).

2. Most case studies in contemporary, psychoanalytically oriented journals include some consideration of these processes. See, for example, Mitchell, 1988, Ogden (1994), Cimino and Correale (2005) and, especially, articles in the journal *Psychoanalytic Dialogues.*

3. Infancy research has documented the transmission of emotional states between mother and infant through study of moment to moment interaction. There is exquisite sensitivity to subtle nuances of affect and infants are shown to be prewired to participate in nonverbal affective communication. See Beebe and Lachmann (1998); Beebe, Lachmann, and Jaffe (1997); Emde (1983); and Tronick (1989). Neuropsychology is also demonstrating the importance of prereflective nonverbal interaction structures as they impact the brain (Schore, 1994).

4. This idea is central to several philosophical and psychological traditions. Postmodernism has brought to the fore this way of seeing the world. In this epistemology, our social worlds are constructed. There is no "objective" reality (Gergen, 1999, Gadamer, 1979). Also, from a rationalist, humanistic perspective, the world is an interpreted environment when people experience it and people imbue their experiences with preexisting meanings (Rychlak, 1988).

5. Winnicott (1975), p. 240. "No human being is free from the strain of relating inner and outer reality . . . relief from this strain is provided by an intermediate area of experience which is not challenged (arts, religion, etc.)."

6. Laing (1969) points out that we also imagine what others think we think about them and what they think we think they think about us.

7. Questionnaire-based social-cognitive research has documented some of the processes by which apparent "negative" traits of a potential mate can be interpreted in a positive way (see Murray and Holmes, 1992) and that people in satisfying and stable relationships assimilate their partners to themselves, "egocentrically" perceiving similarities that were not evident in reality, creating an illusion of having found a kindred spirit (Murray et al., 2002).

8. Melanie Klein originated the concept of projective identification while exploring the paranoid-schizoid position, the tendency of the infant to manage anxiety by splitting good and bad aspects of both self and other. She understood it to be largely an intrapsychic phenomenon where warded-off aspects of self are assigned to an object (in fantasy) and then introjected. Bion (1962) extended her concept to include interpersonal reality by demonstrating how projective identification can be a form of communication in which unmanageable pieces of experience

can be located in another (a container) who will understand, digest the relatively unformed but toxic experience (the contained), and return it in more bearable form. See Joseph (1987) and Ogden (1992) for a particularly clear explication of the distinction and Ogden (1979) for a discussion of the mechanism of projective identification as an interpersonal process. The mechanisms of projective identification were first thought to be limited to psychosis but are now understood to be part of the armamentarium of ordinary defensive functioning, evident both in dyads and in groups. Although initially greeted with skepticism by some classical psychoanalysts, the concept of projective identification, because of its clinical utility, is now well-accepted and widely used in both theory and practice. See Seligman (1999), Aron (1996), Sandler (1987), Ogden (1982), and Grotstein (1981) for theoretical and clinical discussions of projective identification. Family systems theorists and family and couple therapists also find this concept useful. See Dicks (1967), Willi (1984), Middleberg (2001), Catherall (1992), and Scharff and Scharff (1991). Neuropsychoanalysts suggest that projective identification may occur through the work of mirror neurons that imitate what is experienced externally (Greatex, 2002).

9. Psychoanalysts who use the term differ about the balance of intrapsychic and interpersonal processes and the nuances of projection, identification, and containment that are involved in projective identification when one looks closely at the transference/countertransference situation in the analytic session. These technical and theoretical fine points go beyond the scope of the presentation here. See Brunet and Casoni (1996) for a summary of the distinctions.

10. For illuminating examples and discussion of how these processes play out in families and in groups, see Shapiro and Carr (1991) and for a consideration of projective identification in organizations, see Hirschhorn (1988).

11. Apter and Josselson (1998).

12. Mikulincer and Horesh (1999) have shown experimentally that the tendency to project one's own traits onto others varies as a function of attachment style.

13. Ogden (1979). A group of senior psychoanalysts, looking, at a microlevel, at an analytic session, document compellingly the complex relational moves and adjustments that take place between people as they strive for a "fittedness" together. They discuss this in terms of implicit relational knowing that is not available for reflection (Boston Change Process Study Group, 2002).

14. See Ogden (1982) for how this is problematic between therapist and patient and eludes reflection.

15. Social psychologists have demonstrated in the laboratory the ways in which evaluations, decisions, and emotional states occur automatically, without conscious deliberation (Bargh and Chartrand, 1999).

16. See Goffman (1961).

17. See Laing (1967).

18. Existential psychologists and philosophers describe the way in which we co-constitute our world. We create the world that creates us. See Valle and King (1978) and Gergen (1994).

19. See Ricoeur (1992) for a philosophical discussion of these issues.

2

Recreating the
Other in Memory

It is customary in Western cultures to relate one's autobiography as a narrative of agency and achievement—what one has done or tried to accomplish. Relationships with others are generally placed in the background or enter the story as they serve the unfolding of events. A life is conceived as a tale of self-determination—the autonomous self-structuring of one's fate (Eakin, 1999). One can, however, recount one's life story differently, foregrounding relationships that are, after all, inherent to all action. Whatever we do, we do it for, with, because of, or despite someone else. We have no identity at all unless there are others who recognize us as who we believe ourselves to be (Benjamin, 1988).

In life, there are no one-character dramas. Other people inhabit and structure the stages on which our life is enacted. In my research on relationships, I have invited people to tell their life stories through their relationships, noting at each point in their development who were the important people present—in reality and in their minds—and how these other people affected their experience of themselves and their lives. In short, I asked people to tell their lives in terms of what meaning others had for them at each point along the way.

When we read a biography or autobiography, we would be mightily bored with a sequence of events—I went here, did that, then that happened, and so on. What we read for are the interactions with others, the interpersonal tangles that accompanied whatever action took place. This is the stuff of emotional interest in life. As Buber notes, individuality differentiates one from other individualities, but what creates a person is relationships with other persons.

A life told as a relational autobiography sketches the characters who formed the world of the narrator at each point of the life. Who was present, what sort of person they were for the narrator, how they affected him or her—these are the elements that are the essence of a life history. Through such description, we can see the relational world as it "feels" to the narrator.

In this work, I have asked individuals to start by drawing a map of the people who were important to them in their lives beginning at age five, then in five-year intervals up to their current age. On these maps, people can graphically represent how close other people felt to them and how these people were positioned in regard to one another. In addition, people are invited to depict others who were important in their minds but perhaps not physically present—people who had died, for example—and also to draw groups of people where the group itself mattered more than the particular individuals who composed it.[1] I then asked people to tell me at great length about each person on their map, with emphasis on how each person mattered to them and to relate how these meanings may have changed over time.

Over many years, I have sought people in many places and from many walks of life to interview about their relationships. I chose people somewhat randomly, through networking, and I told them that I wanted to learn about how relationships have been important to them in their lives. Earlier, I developed a model of relationships from these interviews (Josselson, 1992). I then began trying to interview people who were prominent in each other's lives and it was to these "linked" interviews that I found myself returning with fascination. Reading these interviews together reminded me of those figures that shift as you look at them, and my musing about them dovetailed with what I knew from clinical work with couples and families and what I know about systems from my work in group relations conferences.[2] People's meaning in each other's lives is not transparent to the players. I therefore wanted to juxtapose these stories and see what we could learn from them—about relationships and about life.

For most people, memories of others are stored as sensations of complex feelings—an aura of how things "were" with that person or what that person was "like." Thinking of people who had been important in their lives, people were often at a loss to come up with specific memories of that person, but it was clear from the expression on their faces that they were remembering the sense of being with them. Memories were organized by feeling rather than events. Trying to call up and describe their mothers, for example, a person might feel suffused with a sense of comfort and warmth and, at the same time, an image of frustration and unfulfilled longing. Or thinking of a particular friend, a person who I interviewed might clearly have an image of that person, an inchoate sense of how it felt to be with them, but language fails to capture the nuances of how one friend "feels" different than another, even if, or perhaps especially when, the activities of the relationship are the same.

My interviewees, then, aided by the maps, often experienced the "sense" or feelings of a relationship first and then called up specific episodes in order to explain to me the basis of their emotional tie. We connect not to the superficial aspects of people but to the deep strata where we experience them to reside emotionally (Mitchell, 1988). Sometimes people could relate an event that seemed to capture the essentials of the bond, a moment that in some sense "stood for" myriad others that in some way defined how it felt to them to be in relationship to this particular other person. In general, relationships are lived more than they are reflected upon.[3] They are the ground of our lives and, like the air that we breathe, we absorb and act on them. Reflection is usually only called into play when there is something problematic afoot—or perhaps when a relationship is new. When we are in conflict with someone important to us, we may focus our attention on the nature of the relationship and perhaps even reflect on whether or not we value the relationship enough to continue participating in it (reflection here being different from fuming or feeling mistreated). Sometimes we reflect on a relationship in hopes of changing its dynamics, and this occurs most often when there is someone with whom to analyze the relationship—a good friend, perhaps, or a therapist. For the most part, people take their relationships as part of the fabric of their lives, the frameworks they live within, the containers for their experience of self.

Looking at and narrating their relationships retrospectively also led people to consider the essence of them. From the distance of time, the images of others that were recalled were the fundamental forms that constituted meaning for them. From the perhaps millions of interactions my interviewees had had with a particular person emerged the persisting core of how the other had mattered. The outer layers having faded with time, the central meanings of the other came more clearly into focus.

Because we as a culture tend to relegate relational experience to the background, our language is limited in being able to express the spectrum of what we might feel and be for others. Words like *love, intimacy,* and *closeness* have so many meanings that it is impossible to know whether you mean anything like what I mean when you use them—unless I ask you a lot of questions that in ordinary social settings would be considered rude. Such words refer to intense emotions but tell us little about what these emotions are like or what evokes them. I still remember that when I was a teenager, my best friend used to tell me about how mean her mother was and, although I spent much time at her house, I never could see anything mean in her warm, caring mother who always made us cookies and then let us do whatever we wanted. I have no doubt, as I had no doubt then, that there was something terrible that my friend experienced with her mother. I listened to her stories, but none of them sounded particularly "mean" to me. What was "mean" to her was simply beyond language—or, at least, her language at the time. Thus, it is a no small matter to tell someone else about *how* relationships have meaning in one's life. And the interviews I conducted often ran to more than four hours as people tried to get language to express complex emotional realities. I was struck by the creativity and courage with which my interviewees struggled to put into words the essences of their experience of others.

In a most general way, people represent others to themselves in terms of the kind of responsiveness they have come to expect from them and the parts of the self that are called out in the relationship. Thus, with one friend, one is prepared to bring one's sense of humor and make jokes, keeping things light, relating the absurd and preposterous moments of life that one has noticed since the last meeting with this friend. Or a lover is recalled in terms of the passion and desire that was aroused, while another evokes memories of quiet moments of comfort and togetherness. Memory has a way of washing off the layers of the relational experience so that only the core meanings remain. "Oh, yes," a person might say, "with Marvin there were also moments of comfortable chat, but what that relationship was really about was sex." Or: "I guess there were times that my mother was loving, but what I really remember was how controlling she was and how I had to always fight her to do anything I wanted to do."

Seldom were people's descriptions of others simple encomiums. Relational stories, like all stories, involve complicating action. People were remembered for their love, support, and encouragement, but people were also remembered as sources of frustration or pain. Sometimes people were depicted as absent, a focus of unfulfilled longing. Taken together, though, each of the people I interviewed was able to communicate to me the terms by which they thought of others, what they experienced of them and wanted from them. I tried to understand the relational experience of each person in the terms they offered to describe their experience, and I did not concern myself with wondering about what the people represented were "really" like. Each person was telling me what these people were like for them—and that is what is most important to me.

When people "create" the characters of their lives, they do so in their essentials and this is what is most remembered and what is remembered most in a emotional way. Because these meanings are closest to the deepest layers of the psyche, these are the ones that are central to the relational glue that binds one person to another. These are the core constructions that shape and sustain the relationship, the ones that, if lost, lead to the collapse of the relationship. Other aspects of the person may be noticed, but not in the same compelling way.

When people tell me about their relationships, then, they are trying to put into language who the important people in their life have been for them in an emotional way, trying to make words carry the subtleties of feeling and unconscious fantasy. These feelings and fantasies govern what they notice about the other. Of the multitude of interactions they have together, of the many layers of traits and ways of being that the other offers, only a few are endowed with psychological significance. And it is through tracing these processes that we can understand better how we create one another.

Because I asked for relational maps at progressive ages, the relational stories I elicited were developmental accounts. Relationships are dynamic entities that change over time as the needs of the actors change and as the external circumstances of life change as well. Thus, I was able to trace the evolution of meanings over time and chart the ebbs and flows of the often contradictory currents. Sometimes my interviewees could account for the changes in narrative form; sometimes they were perplexed by what seemed to just "happen."

The format of the interview and relational mapping frame also allowed me to view the meaning of a particular relationship in the context of a person's other relationships. This is nearly always overlooked in research on relationships that tends to investigate just one relational form—say, with a parent or a romantic partner. But our relationships are always intertwined—our grandmother is intensely important because our mother is detached from us; we move closer to a friend after we get divorced; we were comfortably dependent on a spouse until his father became ill and needed his care, and so on. Our inner relational worlds have many branches and they are interconnected; even what we experience as "just the two of us" is cast against the background of past experience in twosomes.

There are, as is widely recognized, differences between men and women in how they store, remember, and describe relationships. Research has shown that women encode relationships in much greater detail and remember them better and that this is true even at an early age.[4] Women are more attuned to relational shifts and nuances than are men, in part because society engenders in them an attitude of attentiveness to the dynamics of relationships. Women spend more time in conversation trying to "figure out" others, to come to agreement on the proprieties and expectations of others, and to process what others "meant" by what they said and did. Men, in seeming to take relationships at face value, are less likely to reflect on what seems to them self-evident aspects of others and of interactions. In my interviews, I found men no less engaged in relationship but certainly more limited verbally in being able to put into evocative language how others were important to them. But, despite the differences in verbal finesse, I had no reason to believe that relationships are any less central to men than they are to women.

Most of the people I discuss in this book (everyone but Mary and Joan) have been in psychotherapy. Except for Tom and Kathy, who were in therapy with me, I did not know before I interviewed them that they had had this experience. As I chose the stories that seemed best to illustrate the themes I want to bring forward in this book, I gravitated toward those who were most expressive about their experiences. I think that having been in therapy has made these particular people more reflective about their relationships, more able to put into words how others have mattered to them and how their significance has changed as they have grown. I do not think, though, that they differ in any fundamental ways from the many interviewees who had not been in therapy.

All of the relational interviews I conducted were intensely moving—to me and to my interviewees as well. It was clear to me that relationships are where people "live" in the sense that this is the psychic place where intense feelings reside. In the portraits I present in the following chapters, I try to conjure the sense of each person as they are to themselves. But these portraits are, of course, filtered through my own meaning-making, no matter how much I try to keep my own inner self in the shadow. I, too, am engaged in creating the Other. I have chosen to discuss only those people for whom I had strong positive feeling, people I could deeply empathize with, even though this required seeing them both through their own eyes and through the eyes of someone else.

It is difficult not to be judgmental about someone else's relationships—even as a reader. When we hear a relational story, we tend to conclude something, usually something simplistic, about the other's character. This is often why people hesitate to talk to friends about those with whom they are intimate. If Lorna tells Robin, for example, that her husband shouts at her, Robin is likely to draw on the current stock of cultural stories that categorize all things and conclude that Lorna's husband is abusive. "But that's not the whole story," Lorna is left to protest, "there's a lot more to him and to our relationship than that." In other words, the danger is that Robin will assimilate the story fragment to a socially dominant construction rather than try to understand Lorna's experience of her husband.

In the complementary stories that I present here, there are often strong contradictions between the two related people's experiences of events and of the others on their common stage. If we have a realist sensibility, we may wonder what "really" happened. I do not have this sensibility. I believe that memory is always true, but not always accurate. That is, memory reflects a truth of experience, not events. When we remember, particularly when we remember a close relationship, we select from a plethora of moments, interactions, and impressions those that seem to represent the relationship as we have shaped it internally. What we remember is important because it demonstrates those aspects of the relationship that have made the greatest impression on us, in part because they relate to what we were paying attention to in the relationship—and these memories, taken together, outline the "character" as he or she exists on our life stage.

In presenting these people, I have tried scrupulously not to "take sides," which was not very difficult since my interest is in the process by which people construct others. You, the reader, may find yourself taking sides as you read these accounts, and that may give you information about your own tendencies to construct others in certain ways—what draws you, what repels you.

I don't think there is any relational reality of psychological interest beyond what each person makes of it. That is what I wish to explore in this book.

The interpretations I offer about these people and their relationships are for demonstration purposes only and are not "true" of them, although I think they have some accuracy. I make use of these stories to elucidate how the processes of creating the other may work, but a clear understanding of all the dynamic threads that constitute each person would require the kind of scrutiny that is only possible in an analytically oriented psychotherapy. This is the methodological dilemma. Only the contained situation of psychotherapy (or a group relations conference) offers us direct opportunity to observe and reflect on the play of unconscious forces. But if we limit ourselves only to an understanding of the therapeutic relationship, we can overlook how people are engaged in creating the other in everyday life, all the time. Thus, I intend here to show how these particular people *may* be creating one another in hopes that reflection on these psychological processes will allow both therapists and students insight into the often hidden currents of relationships.

NOTES

1. See Josselson (1992) for a complete description of the relational mapping method.

2. Group relations conferences are experiential, temporary institutions in which unconscious group processes are examined in depth. A brief description of the major U.S. conferences sponsored by the A. K. Rice Institute for the Study of Social Systems can be found at www.akriceinstitute.org.

3. See Schutz (1967) for commentary on the relationship between lived experience and reflection.

4. Ross and Holmberg (1992); Acitelli and Holmberg (1993).

3

You Are What I Can't Bear in Myself: Donna and Roberta

In order to survive, we often have to have others to embody what we can't bear to see in ourselves or what in ourselves arouses intolerable anxiety or guilt. We are therefore prone to script into the people closest to us complex ways of being (with us and in the world) that we find unendurable in ourselves. Probably no relationship is closer than that of identical twins. People who grow up intertwined with one another from birth are likely to know each other better than any other pair we could imagine—and the opportunities to create one another are never greater. This is, perhaps, why identical twins are often perceived by others to be opposite to one another in personality—as though they have divided between them available ways to be in the world.

Donna and Roberta, identical twins whom I met when they were thirty-five, demonstrate how entangled a relationship can become when both people are scripting into the other what is difficult to bear in themselves. While doing this resolves some psychological dilemmas, the pain of living with the consequences can also be intense.

DONNA

Donna and Roberta grew up in a poor neighborhood in New York City but now live in Boston. At age thirty-five, Donna writes plays, a few of which have been produced, and teaches theater at a local community college. She is also the single mother of a four-year-old son. Donna spoke in lively, colorful ways, and I experienced her as a passionate, intense

woman who has had many emotionally vibrant relationships with people. Because of her openness and intensity and her dramatic ways of
speaking about herself, I found her enchanting and charming.

Looking back over her life, her identical twin, Roberta, is the person
who has been the constant backdrop of Donna's life, always present in her
mind, and is the first person Donna describes.

"She was an extension of me—whether I wanted it or not, she was
there. We didn't want to dress alike—we always struggled for our own
identity. She was the quiet, good student; I was the rebel—noisy, more
outspoken, more cheerful. We always had the sense that I was the survivor—
that I would be the one to know what to do if something were to happen
to our parents."

But they fought all the time. Still, Donna says, "I couldn't bear to be
apart from her." If they were separated, she felt "like they took my hand
away—her physical presence was a part of my being—I'd feel lost—but
we never had five minutes of peace—we were always fighting. We were
very poor, so we'd fight over the few things we had."

The girls grew up with a regimen of aunts who filled in for the family's
needs, providing food and clothes as well as special treats like going out
for pizza or fun excursions. Donna described her parents as warm and
loving but unable to solve problems or manage well in life. Her mother
was a source of emotional support, love, and tenderness but she was passive and wallowed in being a victim of her life circumstances. Donna's
view of her early family life was that her mother's primary life project
was to change her husband, Donna's father, to try to make something out
of him, a project that never succeeded.

"Most of my mother's energy went to this, then she got too tired and
worn out to do something else. I got this sense that if your parents don't
try to change things for you and make your life better, you're not really
important to them. They always told me I was so beautiful, talented, and
bright, but she never did anything like giving me lessons or taking me to
plays. I've had to learn everything on my own because neither of my parents were models and there was no one to rely on for help with the outside world."

On her map of age five, Donna draws her sister and mother joined, at
the same distance from her as her father. Donna adored her father who
she feels loved her more than he did her sister. He loved her joyfulness
and playfulness. While Roberta seemed to be "symbiotic" (in Donna's
view) with their mother, Donna had a special relationship with their father. However, this was before she understood who he was in the world.
"I loved him, I admired his brilliance—and I didn't know of the terrible
things he was doing." Donna described her father as a "lunatic Bohemian.
He ran away from everything all the time. He saw the family as tempo-

rary, something that would eventually be over." There was, she felt, a strong love story between her parents based on his being the *enfant terrible*, while her mother took the strong, martyred position of being right all the time. When Donna was ten, the family moved to New Jersey and her father decided to take a salaried job. He became the provider at this point, at least for a while. Donna says that when he became responsible, "my mother died from this, became a vegetable. Her reason for existence was to scold him." In Donna's depiction of her parents, we already see the traces of the counterbalancing between opposites and the ways in which one can need someone to be what one, at another level, does not want. Donna perceives that her mother needed her father's irresponsibility even as she detested him for it and suffered from it.

During her childhood, theirs was a happy house where friends and neighbors would come to listen to music and to have fun. Donna felt intensely close to her father although he embarrassed her from time to time. "I felt very close but never really took him seriously. I was fantasizing and pretending he was my man—but he was not really someone I really admired. I admired his intelligence and sense of humor, but he was still not at all responsible or dependable. We would have good times talking and laughing but then he would disappear." Remembering her life at age ten, she drew herself and her father as a connected unit, while mother and Roberta were joined together nearby. Donna reveled in her father's liveliness much as her mother had, but all the while had to cope with her longings for someone to depend on. Identified, perhaps, with her father's impulsivity and independence, she, at least, did not want to join what seemed like a suffocating togetherness between Roberta and their mother. This left her allied with an undependable parent.

With Roberta, closeness was taken for granted as something given in life and inevitable. Whatever else they did, they were still fundamentally joined as a unit. "I always had more friends than she did—sometimes I'd go off with my friends and she'd be really hurt." So, having friends wasn't just having friends, but implied hurting Roberta's feelings. Everything she did had implications for Roberta who was always watching, reacting, and measuring herself against Donna. The struggle to feel separate from Roberta and pull away from the almost irresistible oneness was central to Donna's emotional life.

Adolescence, as for many people, was a terrible time for Donna. As her body began to grow and develop, Donna became what she described as a "compulsive eater" and gained a lot of weight. She felt that she was fat and her hatred of the way she looked colored all of her relationships, but particularly with Roberta. She was envious and felt she was losing some kind of race between them. Although they looked alike, she began to think of Roberta as the pretty one.

"I had nothing to feel good about myself for, no sense of myself. My sister at least was a better student—I felt I had no parents, no special or particular friends, boys didn't want me—I just read and ate—I had no sense of being." When Donna perceived Roberta's beauty and accomplishment, her envy produced even more misery.

When the girls were nineteen, their mother died and, for Donna, everything seemed to fall apart. "When I look at pictures of her, she was always leaning on people. She was warm, needing love. She was also a wonderful listener—good at sitting in a chair and listening to people and their problems, so people adored her. When she died, my father became completely bizarre. No one came to visit any more. After Roberta got married, I left home and moved in with Roberta and Roberta's husband, Will, for a month. I felt completely and entirely alone. I felt like the two of us are alone in the world. Well, Will was there, but it was still really the two of us."

At age twenty, Donna became enamored of Bert, who had dated Roberta when they were in high school. "But I never let anything romantic develop because he had dated my sister." Then he became seriously ill and Donna stayed by his bedside all the time. "He was very complicated, very closed. We only discussed literature and movies. He has become a well-known writer, and three years ago he dedicated a short story to me and told me how much I had meant to him over these years, but he had never told me before. It was a revelation that I had been something important to him. To me, he was the brother I never had." More than this, though, Bert represented for Donna the first important person who was really different from her, the first person she could in no way experience as a part of herself—although he was still colored in her mind by his connection to Roberta.

Donna's first real boyfriend, Marty, was wildly in love with her and although she didn't really love him, she enjoyed his romantic adoration of her. Donna was working in "a mindless secretarial job" in New York City and got involved with the feminist movement. Her friend Yvonne encouraged her to go to college and helped her figure out how to get a scholarship. "That became a wonderful year—age twenty. I discovered I had a mind. I loved it that teachers expected you to think for yourself and do work on your own. I discovered that I loved to study and loved to spend hours in the library—I did so well, I became the best student in the department." One of her aunts seemed to take her mother's place and would come over to her student apartment with groceries and do things for her.

Looking back to this age, twenty, Donna says little about Roberta, although she draws Roberta nearest to herself on the map. She was very much there, but in the background, a kind of safe but conflictual potential haven from the world. Donna's struggle to differentiate herself and find a unique self continued through the threads of feminism and men. She had an affair with a professor. She formed an intimate friendship with one of her women teachers, Myra, and she, Roberta, and Myra did a book together. Donna doesn't comment on getting Roberta involved in the project she was doing with Myra, taking for granted that Roberta would be able to enter wherever she went. Donna found people at this stage of her life to value her, to "build my ego" and buttress her intellectual ambitions. "These people really took an interest in me, wanted to know about me, and what was happening to me—I really developed intellectually." Still, she felt alienated, like she didn't really belong anywhere. Looking back, despite the bright spots, she remembers the period from ages twenty to twenty-five as a "terrible time."

By the time she reaches age twenty-five in her story, Donna takes up her narrative by contrasting her life with Roberta's. "I was doing what I wanted and she was fulfilling duties—she had a baby when we were twenty-five." Donna could construct her identity in counterpoint to Roberta—she was free; Roberta was fettered. Donna's emotional life was dominated by Myra, who had become an intimate friend. "She was very feminist, she mesmerized me. I was in love with her. I admired her. I think we were in love for a long time. She felt I was so bright and wonderful and that I would go so far. She and another professor of mine really gave me the courage to try to do something, to go for the master's program. Myra was the opposite of my mother. She'd say, 'You're so bright' and get me a scholarship—or 'You're so bright' and give me a high grade." Donna had one sexual experience with Myra. "It really messed up the relationship. I discovered I'm not a lesbian. I don't know if I did it to please her. I never repeated it and it left such a scar on our friendship. We didn't have the guts to talk about it. Then she left the country for many years. Later she told me she had been in love with me but was wounded when I told her it wasn't my thing."

Later in her twenties, Donna also had an affair with Sherman, who "built up my ego as a woman. He worshipped me, he loved me. I was so much younger, looked good and the fact that I could love him made him feel good. He was charming and good-looking and that built me up. But he's an alcoholic. He still thinks of me, and he told me that I am the passion of his life. He wasn't someone I could really respect, but he did wonders for my ego." She also had an affair with Charles, another of her professors. "We had sex, but it wasn't important. The intellectual side was very important. We had a strong intellectual rapport."

These people, Donna said, really took an interest in her and helped her to develop intellectually, but she was still feeling alienated. "My friends were my teachers. I would go to gatherings with them but I wasn't a teacher and didn't belong. The feeling of not having a sense of who I was still continued."

At age twenty-eight, Donna finished her master's degree in theater, and the first significant step she took on her own was to move to Boston to take a job that she felt was right for her. It was also her first geographical move away from Roberta. There, Donna met and fell in love with Harry and married him. It didn't take long for Roberta to follow her to Boston. A year later, Roberta left Will, and Will and their daughter Jennifer moved in with Donna and Harry. Donna took care of Jennifer while Roberta did what she wanted to do, staying with all of them occasionally. On Donna's map of this age, they all intersect and overlap. For unexplained reasons, Donna at this point tried to offer Roberta some of the freedom that had previously been hers alone, but the old balance soon restored itself.

Harry was a handsome, charming dreamer. He engaged in wildly optimistic but doomed business ventures or simply stopped working. At a deeper level, Donna's relationship with Harry had overtones of her relationships with both her father and with Roberta. Like her father, he was charming but unpredictable and disappointing, and like her early relationship with Roberta, they fought all the time. "I knew he was a lunatic and fucked up but I needed to repeat the pattern. I married him knowing that I'd divorce him and yet we had a great sex life and he loved me a lot."

After her marriage, Donna nevertheless remained intensely involved with her women friends. Like Donna, her new friends were self-reflectively trying to grow and overcome past struggles. Most were in the theater world or were artists. They shared their intellectual passions and creative pursuits. These were friends she believed would be with her throughout her life. She emphasized the intensity of these relationships, which were engaging both intellectually and in terms of sharing experiences and exploring life together.

Today, at age thirty-five, Donna no longer draws herself in the center of her map. "I no longer feel in the center with the whole world around me. I had had this incredible arrogance that made up for all the insecurity I had felt. I didn't even want to go into therapy because I thought it was the world that was wrong, not me. Now I see myself as a series of things—a worker, a mother, a sister, an ex-wife. I accept people and situations a lot more easily. My becoming a mother has been such a redeeming experience for me in the sense that it's taught me how to give without expecting anything in return and has taught me my own limitations. I used to be full of impatience and wanting instant gratification and instant love, instant orgasm, now I feel more able to wait, to be patient. Having Alec has taught me to accept my limitations. At age twenty-five, I would have resented him for that, but it happened at a time that I could learn about ap-

preciating otherness and that people are not just extensions of my own being, my own fucked-upness, my own experiences with my parents. A lot
of that was that he was born a boy—I had this weird experience when he
was born—I felt I was giving birth to myself—something so new was being created, something so new in me was coming out. One of my most serious problems was all the splits I had. I had to work on how to integrate
things, get the opposites to coexist.

"I couldn't see myself as both an independent, intellectual woman and
someone who makes a cup of coffee for her husband. Right after I gave
birth, the second day, I felt my breasts engorged—the most physical experience I ever had in my life. I was so full and heavy and loving it. I was
fat and didn't feel uncomfortable with my body. I began writing, felt
together—going through an incredible physical experience and writing
about it—physical glue that put me together—everything I've done since
he was born was out of this feeling—he's really taught me to accept myself, with my limitations and my strengths.

"At this time, Roberta felt to me like a strong ghost. It's okay if she
leaves me, moves somewhere else. I no longer feel it would be unthinkable for her to be apart from me. Things were so tense between us—but
I'm very attached to Jennifer, and Jennifer and Alec are attached. I see in
Roberta everything I don't like to remember about me."

Donna said that she didn't admire Roberta and didn't want to emulate
her—not in her marriage, not as a mother. "She doesn't know how to relate to me like a separate person. We were so caught in the pattern that she
was right and I was wrong and she was mothering me, and now the pattern is not that. She hasn't really done anything better than I have. I think
she envies me for not compromising, for having wonderful friends.

"I love Will dearly, I think he's wonderful but he's too much under her
influence. I had a messy separation from Harry. His business went bank-
rupt and he left terrible debts. Then I had an accident and was half-crip-
pled, with a baby, but I wanted Harry out of my life so badly. All the time
we had been married, we were never friends, but now we are. I can trust
him as the father of my child and turn to him for help and he will help me,
and I show him a lot of appreciation. I've really learned to relate to people as really separate human beings. I never throw the past up to him, you
have to allow people to change. I'm enjoying our being friends—this is so
much better than being at each other's throats."

Donna has stayed close with her woman friends, talking to one on the
phone every day, seeing another, who is far away, every few months. She
has also reintensified her friendship with Bert, who is "just starting to
play around with the idea of my being a woman. There is a new element
to the friendship due to changes in him, a new intimacy. It's lovely, I'm enjoying it."

As she narrates her relational autobiography, Donna portrays herself as a person who has been very focused on her own personal and intellectual growth and, throughout her life, has been drawn to people who seem able to teach her something or appreciate her for her talents or her femininity. Donna has been in search of others not to take care of her but to "build up" her sense of self. She falls in love easily, with friends as well as lovers, and longs for people who encourage her to stretch and enlarge herself and to be creative. For her, Roberta has been an ever-present but irritating twin sister, someone Donna has had to fight all her life in order to become herself. Roberta has been the "good" girl she has had to try to find a comfortable distance from, a shadowy figure whom she cannot in any way idealize or learn from. Roberta seems always to be in the wings, takes a role now and then, as when she works on the book with Donna and Myra or moves to Boston after Donna marries. In some ways, Donna doesn't really notice Roberta or what may be the story of her life. She appears without exactly being called and then Donna needs to get away from her again. Donna needs her nearby but also finds her presence intolerable and suffocating to her own individuality.

In some important ways, we can't "know" Roberta at all through Donna's portrait of her. Donna has created her as a foil to herself, but Roberta also represents a kind of stability and constancy through Donna's passionate adventuring. Donna seems to wish her there as a presence that she doesn't actually have to look at too directly—a kind of home she can always return to, however ambivalently. As Donna puts it in her last reflection on their relationship, Roberta has been "a strong ghost." As with a ghost, Donna is not so much in relationship with Roberta as an independent, separate person, but with what she represents to her. Donna says, "I see in Roberta everything I don't like to remember about me." From this, we understand that Roberta resides in an imaginary space within Donna, embodying all the characteristics she wishes to disown in herself. Still, Donna's illusion is that Roberta is, as she said, like her hand—a part of her, a loved and hated part that she has to keep both attached and distant.

We note, however, that Donna says, at age thirty-five, "I no longer feel it would be unthinkable for her to be apart from me," thus acknowledging that it *had* once been unthinkable. Donna's assumption had been that Roberta would always be there, tied to her in some way, so that she could keep trying to get away. In almost an offstage whisper, Donna mentions that Roberta had been "mothering" her, but she says this in a way that suggests that she didn't consciously want such mothering. She is also able to acknowledge that Roberta's strengths, although she could count on them, made her envious; thus, she has to recount to herself all that she despises in Roberta. She cannot both admire Roberta and sustain her pleasure in her own qualities and achievements.

Although it is always suspect to summarize such a complex relationship, we might say that what Donna has created in Roberta is a person who must always be there so she can struggle to get away from her. The formula is something like, "I feel most myself when I know myself to be most different from you and I need you there trying to keep me from being me. And I need you there so that if I feel myself failing or falling, you will still be there and I won't be alone."

ROBERTA

But who is Roberta? Is she indeed a bit player who appears when Donna needs her, happily playing the foil to Donna's emerging talented self, being the continent that Donna can sever herself from? This is not very likely.

I found Roberta, at age thirty-five a highly successful computer consultant who travels frequently in her work, to be a soft-spoken, somewhat reserved, but warm and engaging woman. It was somewhat disconcerting for me to meet Roberta because she looks and sounds so much like Donna, although Donna's hair is long and loose while Roberta's is stylishly cut short. One of them has added color to her hair, most likely Donna. They are not so much alike that side by side they would be difficult to tell apart, but the resemblance is very strong.

More introverted than Donna, Roberta is not nearly so flamboyant but has a quiet intensity—and is equally insightful and psychologically aware. Her language is more understated, but her strong feelings as she narrated the struggles of her life made me feel very sympathetic toward her. Roberta related a parallel story of an intense journey to personal growth. Her sister Donna has been a major figure throughout her life, but in a very different way than Roberta was important for Donna.

Roberta's relational maps are striking in that, in all of her drawings, her own circle, representing herself, is drawn as a circle within a larger circle, a subpart of others' lives, indicating that she experiences herself not as distinct and separate but as part of a larger unit. At age five, she is part of a complex circle that includes her mother, father, and sister. This continues until age twenty-five, when the circle of which she is a part includes herself, her husband and daughter, her sister, and the lingering imagined presence of her mother. Only when she draws the relational map she would wish for in five years (something she offered to do) does she draw herself as a bounded circle, with lines connecting her to others. Mother remains a "ghost" on her current map of age thirty-five.

Donna, by contrast, draws herself as a separate circle, usually larger than all the others, until age thirty, when she draws her circle as overlapping and intersecting those of her husband and sister, with Will (her sister's husband) overlapping the other two. By age thirty-five, in her current relational picture, her circle is once again separate but now smaller than the others. Throughout, Donna puts many more people on her map than Roberta— friends and colleagues. Neither parent is on Donna's map after age fifteen.

Roberta, reflecting on her early life at age five, describes her inner life as dominated by her mother. "She was so important that I felt that I didn't have any existence. I was so close to her that I had this constant fear that anything that might happen to her would leave me without a life of my own. When I was five, I had this dream that she was dead and ever since then, I had this constant fear about what would become of me." Roberta felt her mother "was the kind of mother that would be taken for granted. We were her whole life. Our financial situation was miserable and she was constantly in a battle for providing us with food. Every night she'd say, 'what am I going to feed you tomorrow?'" Aunts and uncles were important because they brought food. Her mother would feed herself with the leftovers. Roberta wonders if their poverty was part of creating so much of her anxiety about what might happen tomorrow. She worried that they were an economic burden. "If we hadn't been there, it would have been easier for her. That made it hard for us to enjoy life." They lived in a one-bedroom apartment. Mother and the two girls shared a room while their father slept on the sofa in the living room. They had no toys. "We didn't even have a corner of our own, let alone a room of our own. I felt that no matter what I did I did not have any room to even have a chance to see who I was or what I was or what I wanted."

Roberta describes her relationship with her sister as "very close and symbiotic." "Donna was the one who wanted things, who asked. Mom never wanted anything—it was wrong to ask for anything because there was nothing to give. So to be a good child was to give up altogether any wish or will or aspiration. It wasn't until I gave birth to Jennifer that I had the feeling that if I wanted to create an independent strong-willed child, I would have to learn to want things and learn how to accomplish things and I realized how wrong it was for me not to want anything or not to wish for anything and that it was morally right to want and it wasn't easy. I'm still not free from it even today. Guilt was the dominant feeling in my life. It was so hard on my family for us to be alive." In Roberta's mind, then, Donna was the one who wanted, perhaps wanting on behalf of them both, in order to relieve Roberta of her intense guilt over wanting since wanting would cause their mother to suffer even more.

In the face of the external deprivation, Roberta describes herself as having had a rich fantasy life. "I was very withdrawn, barely uttered a word until I was seventeen. I was the good kid in the house, my grades were fine. I put so much energy into being good, not allowing myself to want. I was so anxious all the time. Until late in my life, I wasn't even aware that I had any thoughts or that I could create anything."

Roberta describes her relationship with Donna as "very close in the sense that we could not be apart. When we were still at home, if one of us would get sick, the other one might be sent over to my aunt, but we would be on the phone all day talking. But when we were together we were constantly fighting over anything. I remember us like one person, very different in temperament but we were together all the time. I never had any friends. She was all my life, but she would have friends—she was the social part, more outgoing, easy to make friends with—I was anxious, full of anxieties, nightmares, very little hope for anything becoming better—I was very unhappy."

Her father was not very important in her life. "He was causing a lot of misery to my mother. They were fighting a lot. He would be there with all of those friends they were constantly having over. He taught us some things—I just didn't feel he could shape my life or influence it in any way. He was very remote, in the background. But he was very close to my mother. She couldn't do without him. He wasn't a provider so I couldn't understand why she was so dependent on him, wouldn't leave him. I was very close to her but she was close to him. Donna was much closer to him—that was important for her. I was my mother's daughter and she was my father's daughter. After my mother died, it was hell. He would disappear from our lives altogether. Donna had a harder time with it which just intensified my feelings about having to take care of her."

From an early time, Roberta also depicts aunts and uncles who doted on them, provided food, movies, and motorcycle rides. When the twins were ten, they moved in with their maternal grandmother and her sister, but their grandmother died shortly afterward. "My mother was constantly concerned with who else could be responsible for her children. My aunt Laura took charge of us. For me it was a nightmare. She was so bitchy and critical. She'd just make our lives miserable telling us what to do, how to do it, punishing us. Later we moved to where another of her sisters was living and that was a wonderful place, heaven on earth." During this time, their father was working and the girls had a room of their own.

With Donna, though, Roberta was "fighting like crazy because she had all these friends and I didn't. She would reject me when she had a friend around and I would have to be left alone. On the one hand, I felt she was constantly needing me and I felt I was being rejected and I didn't understand why she needed anybody else if she had me. I felt I couldn't be without her and it seemed so easy for her to go out and make friends and not need me."

As a teenager, Roberta was intensely miserable and thought a lot about wanting to die. "I felt incompetent, rejected. I wasn't sure if I even existed—I felt I was reaching the depths of not being." Part of this was that everyone else seemed to be having boyfriends. She began eating compulsively and grew fat. "If I made an attempt to make a girlfriend she would end up being Donna's friend. I couldn't manage to do anything on my own. I didn't stand any chance in competing with her in that realm. My strong points were having good grades so that I could remain the goody-goody in the family. My sister allowed herself to fail. So grades were my strong point that would make me separate from her but school wasn't a good experience. I didn't really see it as something I could gain anything from. My feeling was one of not being there. I had this constant feeling that out there was a world that I could not reach."

At age fifteen, Roberta was still "terrorized" by her aunt Laura. "My mother knew how badly she treated us but it was like we were the taxes she was paying for all the help my aunt had given her over the years. My mom didn't have a will of her own. She felt stuck with this relationship." Aunt Bea and uncle Bill remained for Roberta the fun part of life, offering happy moments amid all the gloom and worry.

At the time when her mother died when she was nineteen, Roberta had still felt she "was my whole life. But the amazing thing I found out when she was actually dead was how well I could do without her. But I was very angry that at the point where I didn't need her as a mother but could really be a friend, then she died and I felt abandoned. But I think this was the first step in my growing process, finding my powers, what I was capable of."

Roberta's first experience of herself and her potential occurred when Donna went to college in a different city. "For the first time in my life we were separated, and I could begin to find myself in some ways. I felt that the more I separate from her, the more I can allow myself to be what I want to be and what I really am and not feel guilty all the time that whatever I do it's at somebody's expense. Since my mother died it's been a struggle for independence, learning to lean on myself and not carrying the ancient history of being constantly guilty no matter where I go or what I do. Even now, for me to tell Donna 'no' is something I can't do. My immediate feeling is I feel so guilty, how can I tell her 'no.' After mother died, I became responsible for my sister. She took her time to grow up and I felt that I had to be her mother and I wasn't allowed to make any mistakes. My mother created this myth that Donna was the irresponsible kid. I was the responsible one, my mother would turn to me. I had to finish the chores. I would iron Donna's things, do the laundry, cook for her. My mother was already sick—at that time, there was no question that I had to do it—she would expect me to do it and I expected myself to do it—she was so dependent on me and these services that I was supplying and I was feeling dependent on her dependence on me and there was no way to break free."

Roberta didn't leave for college because their mother was dying "and one of us had to remain home to look after her. It was only natural that I would remain home. Donna was miserable away at school and said if I didn't come there, she would throw herself into the sea. I'd take the bus to see her, called her every night to see how she was doing. I realized that as long as my sister was miserable, I couldn't be happy. The next year, I went to Vassar, where Donna was, and although my first year at Vassar was good, I couldn't be happy without feeling very guilty. I had also lost a lot of weight and looked very beautiful. For the first time I really experienced my beauty and power of attraction. Boys started to fall in love with me— that really built my confidence with the other sex. Since I had such a remote relationship with my father, the other sex was so remote and unreachable. In high school the very first relationship I had with a boy was a love relationship. He was madly in love with me, and although I felt wanted and desired, and that was nice, after a short while I wanted out of it. Then I had a frustrating experience with Bert, someone I cared for a lot and he cared for me a lot, but we were both so inhibited that we couldn't do much together and at some point, I broke it off. Later he became one of Donna's best friends. I experienced this as another taking away. I still feel strongly connected to him as well. Donna was being the problem all the time. I felt that the moment I would start getting closer to him, it would create a competition and I couldn't stand competing with her over anything. So if she took something away from me, it was taken away and that was that. At this age, she was fat and I was thin. I was looking great and she would cut my clothes and steal my makeup. She was so jealous."

Roberta had met Will at age nineteen and married him at twenty-one. "One of the reasons I got married so young was so I wouldn't need anybody. For me the most frustrating and desperate feeling is to be dependent. I have to have my own car, my own salary. I can't stand to be dependent." At the outset, Will seemed to her to be caring and affectionate. He brought her flowers and spent nights with her at the hospital while her mother was dying. So when he asked her to marry him, she said yes. After the honeymoon, he became distant and difficult to talk to. Their sex life was frustrating. Roberta, however, was so much involved with Donna and her hardships and miseries and pain at being abandoned by their father who threw her out of the house that she had little energy for paying much attention to Will. She felt she tried, in some sense, to make Donna their child. Donna was with them all the time.

When Roberta went to Vassar, she and Donna took all their courses together. Even when they were no longer living under the same roof, Donna came every night to be with them. This went on until they were twenty-five. When Jennifer was born, she felt to Roberta very much like a *second* child.

Roberta still misses her mother and wishes her mother could see her married and being a mother herself and be proud of her for how successful she is in her work. "Mostly I miss her when I feel I cannot break away from my sister because that would be to betray her. I was the competent one for my sister. Nothing I couldn't do or cope with, I could get her out of all her problems. I felt very powerful over her and her life—complete feeling of control—terrible feeling that I couldn't afford to lose control for one second but also feeling that having that much control is not so good. I had the feeling that she really couldn't do without me and I wasn't willing to give that up until I turned thirty.

"I wanted her to acknowledge all that I went through with her and I felt I couldn't really get away from her until she did that. Only recently I became emotionally willing to give up any demands on her recognition of this. I just don't want that anymore. Now I just want the air between us to be clear. I don't care any more about what she did to me or what I did to her and why. I had to experience myself as a real bitch to step out of the trap I was in all those years. In her experience, I was always better off. Her relationships with men were not so successful. In her view, I was always more than her.

When I got separated from Will, I gave everything away so that I wouldn't have more than Donna. I felt I had to be as "without" as she. I had to be equal in order to separate from her. I couldn't stand telling her to go to hell when I had so much more than her— a house, a husband, and beautiful possessions—how could I tell her to go to hell when her husband abandoned her with a baby? I allowed Will to join Harry in a business partnership even though I knew it was going to be a disaster and I knew we would lose everything. We had to pay the debts. I had to sell my apartment to pay Harry's debts. So that now that I was screwed up also, I could separate from her. I really hope that today at this stage in my life, I could build a future including having good things without feeling guilty."

For all Roberta's tendencies to merge with others, she had an unusual experience of pregnancy and birth. After a difficult pregnancy, Jennifer was born by Caesarean. "I never experienced her as a part of me even during my pregnancy. I experienced this totally separate person growing inside of me. She doesn't look like me. When I gave birth—feeling that I didn't have a natural birth—she was brought to me next day—it was like she had been brought to me from the outside and for me that signified the desperate need for separation. I didn't want her to be a projection of me or what I never was or what I wanted to be. And this was a projection of my need and desire to experience my sister as coming to me from the outside as an equal and not to suck on me because of all the needs and holes that she has. I wanted her to come to me as a complete person who would give me what she wanted to give. This enabled me to raise Jennifer by letting her be.

"If you look at her, she is so much herself—she is not me or Will—she is so *separate*. I don't feel that she is my daughter in the sense that she has to carry on anything in me and I have this feeling with her that our relationship changes—at times it's good, at times it's great. It's like having a relationship with somebody, a relationship that you have to work on because it's not to be taken for granted. She's warm and loving and caring, a real giver but she also knows what she wants and how to get it, knows how to speak her mind—so in that sense she is what I wanted her to be— also a reflection of what I wanted to achieve with my sister and my mother. I realized how wrong my relationship with my mother was and what it had done to me and how it had affected me.

"When we moved to Boston, where Donna was, I felt I had to do something if I wanted my relationship with Donna to change. I didn't want to be a mother to her anymore. At one point I just stopped bringing her food. This was my first step toward a different relationship with her.

"My mother was still present in the sense of how different I wanted to be from her, how wrong it was not to have anything of your own. For the first time in my life, I craved making mistakes, being able to be wrong. I had my first affair and had to break up with Will because it was inconceivable to have another relationship and be married.

"At age twenty-nine, my relationship with Will was very frustrating. He was distant and we still had a crummy sex life. I looked very good at that age and I was taking literature courses. I felt my femininity and sexuality blooming and I felt that it was legitimate to take a lover. But I had to break up with Will first. I also began to feel that there were more important things in life than being a mother and I sent Jennifer to live with Will in New York for three months. Jennifer had no place in my life at that point— I wanted her out of my life. For once in my life, I had a need to let go.

"For three months, I had a relationship with a black man, Leroy, who was everything I ever wanted from a man—intelligent, bright, passionate. We became lovers and I was swept away and overwhelmed by this passion. I hadn't ever felt this before, to find in one person everything I would look for. Had he not been black, I might have. . . .

"I had other relationships, but although these people were very crucial in my development, I didn't experience them as people who could be part of my life in the way Donna was or Will was. With Will, I had this feeling of common fate. I'm so attached to Will that I don't think that, like with Donna, no matter how much we could hate each other or scream at each other or wish that the other one had never been born, on the other hand I also feel that she will always be there. She is so much a part of me emotionally. When I go abroad, I miss her and feel my love for her, and the intense feelings of anger and hate just disappear. Here's this person who I just love so much and can't be separated from. With Will it's the same. No matter how much I hate him and feel that his incompetence won't allow him to be what I want him to be, somehow he will always be part of my life.

"After we separated, he had a girlfriend and I couldn't stand the idea that he would be out of my life. With Leroy, I knew I had to put an end to it because he was black. And I felt I couldn't put Jennifer through it."

Around this time, Roberta met Pam, who became her best friend. Pam was also going though a crisis with her marriage and struggling to function as the mother of a two-year-old. Roberta describes herself as "falling in love" with Pam and developing an intense relationship in which they could tell each other everything. "We have been growing as persons in this friendship and the friendship has been growing and what I cherish mostly in this friendship is that it's not a friendship of—its something I always wanted in a relationship—that the person I am with really sees me and what I need, not just a projection of her needs and what she wants. If I would say something about Will, she'd see Will in his relationship with me and not the fact that she was having a hard time with her husband and so separation was a good thing. It was a relationship of being very close but still objective about each other. She was the first person in my life who loved me for what I was and not for what I was providing. I could allow myself to be wrong with her. I could expose the dark side of me."

With Jennifer, after the separation, Roberta described herself as having "an animal like feeling. I just wanted to be with my daughter, and felt I no longer had the energy to be with Leroy. Will had an apartment close by so he could see her. I wanted to be left alone to be Jennifer's mother. I felt guilty for having abandoned her for those couple of months, and felt I had to make it up to her.

"At this point, Donna is out of my life in the sense that she feels that I need support and she can't give it to me. I was on my own, trying to cope with everything. We had an argument; she couldn't offer me any help. She only wanted me to give to her."

After six months of separation, Roberta reunited with Will. Still good friends, Roberta largely gave up on having a sexually satisfying marriage but nevertheless entered therapy. "I also felt I had to make it up to Will for leaving him and make it up to Jennifer for the separation so I went to work for Will and I loathed it. Getting back with Will was giving up on my womanhood, I looked terrible, couldn't care less about how I looked and I was just Jennifer's mother. I would stay up with her for hours helping her with schoolwork and I felt I had to be there with her. Working for Will allowed me to be home when Jennifer was home and I felt I didn't have the energy of making any commitment. After some months of this, which felt like years, I realized I had to face reality and get out of Will's business company, and I got another job which was a first step toward being appreciated again, having a decent job again with interesting, independent, and creative work where I could use my skills. The relationship with Will changed a lot. It improved in that we became good friends. He was a good guy and a great father to Jennifer and in life one has to compromise. So he's not the greatest lover, but so what—he has these other qualities."

A few years ago, when the legal and economic aftermath of Will's involvement with Harry hit home, Roberta decided to sell her apartment to bail everyone out—and keep Will from possibly going to jail. "I saw him not coping very well and I had to do a lot of the taking loans and filing suit. I had to put so much energy into these things, appearing in courtrooms, before judges—not exactly something that made me feel comfortable. I began to experience with Will what I had experienced with Donna—that if I didn't become involved in what's happening, then it's a disaster. I felt I couldn't have complete confidence in him, I couldn't trust him with making a good decision. He was pretending it wasn't happening. Finally, I sold my apartment to pay all those debts and I was very disillusioned with him, realizing I couldn't have confidence in him."

Around this time, Roberta started an affair with a married man, an affair that had near-disastrous consequences. "I felt very guilty—not so much guilty towards Will, more towards Donna because there she is alone, she doesn't have anybody. There I am—I have a husband and a lover and she has no one. She had even said, 'Don't think about me.' This was the most reassuring thing toward making the decision to have the affair. We were meeting at Donna's apartment and at some point it became very difficult for her. Her tone was that I was taking too much for myself. But eventually I fell in love with him, and emotionally he became the center of my life. All my energy went into it—both the passion and the effort to avoid guilt. He's very successful, has lots of money, is a great lover— very successful, knows how to treat a woman, very much what I needed at this time in my life. I became pregnant by him. I let myself become pregnant—the fact that I allowed it to happen. . . . He gave me money for an abortion. It was a traumatic experience. I bled for a whole month. Will knew nothing about it. I had to go to the hospital and Will brought me flowers. The relationship became very painful and I wanted out of it. I felt like my whole life is a lie, I'm lying to everybody. I felt the abortion was the price I had to pay for having the affair and it became clear to me that as much as I wanted to be the kind of person who could occasionally have an affair and so what, it just isn't my personality. I was so traumatized by the pregnancy and abortion, not the end of the relationship with my lover. When we meet today, I feel nothing toward him.

"With Donna, ever since Alec was born, I decided consciously to get out of her life. We got into a separation process, each with the help of therapy. The main issue was how do you do it and stay alive and not die of guilt. It was very hard in the beginning. For her, it was the first time in her life that she started hating me, could express a lot of hate. She had an accident that crushed her leg, she had a six-month-old baby and her husband just left her and I was leaving her, too, making a decision to leave her. Not long ago she accused me of throwing her to the dogs—not true, I had found her a babysitter before I left and dropped by each day to make sure everything was okay—but I also experienced it as throwing her to the dogs—my therapist was crucial in helping me see that what I was doing was not so wrong. This process is still going on. With time, my sister becomes more independent, more able to control her life, doesn't need me so much. It's like a child telling himself he can do it on his own without his parents behind him—and sometimes she would do this with a lot of love and understanding and sometimes she would do it with a lot of hate and resentment."

Roberta and Will are planning to move to Florida. She sees it as a new life, a new beginning. "Some days I'm consumed with guilt. I find myself in little ways giving up my will in favor of Donna's wishes and needs—going to a movie when I was sick but she wanted to go. I knew I felt like I have to make it up to her for my moving—anything that entails something good for me and something bad for her makes me feel so guilty. My immediate feeling is I have to make it up to her. Some people have fantasies of winning the lottery—mine is of winning enough millions to give some to each other person so I can enjoy my share—that's what I most wish to change in my life."

Of Jennifer at this age, Roberta says, "I'm not a very good mother—not very patient—I find it hard to do with her things I don't like doing. Will will do anything, play anything with her. She matters to me. The day she was born I stopped needing to write poetry (I had published some)—my poems had been very pessimistic and I felt I couldn't be that kind of person any more and Jennifer signified all the joy I had in me and all the love in my life—love of music and dance, all the positive energy I had in me and never found an outlet for it—it was a sense that she was the creation of my life so what did I need to write poems for. I was so afraid that she would get into something like the relationship I had with my mother that I went to the other extreme of letting her be Jennifer and she is, she is so strongly herself. That prevented me from sometimes getting closer to her. I was afraid I would be too much for her. But I can't tell you how important she is to me. I have such a strong feeling that she would always be safe because of my love for her. It was a real trauma when I realized that she, too, is vulnerable. I have terrible fits of anxiety about this. I feel I couldn't survive life without her."

At present, still in Boston preparing for their move, Roberta and Will are in therapy together. She feels that they are making a lot of progress and that finally he's become a great lover. "I'm happy to be with him and share my life with him." At present, Donna is out of the circle. "For a couple years, I really kept her out of my life. There was lots of animosity between us—we couldn't communicate at all—she felt I was trying to keep her out of my relationships with new friends, that I would never invite her. Today things are very different. We've made a lot of progress, but in the last month, what I believe truly is that for each one of us to do best, the best thing is to live in two separate towns—she doesn't drive so I have to drive her and she doesn't have money for babysitters so I have to help."

Roberta remains close to her best friend, Pam, who remains, for her, "a model of growth." She feels that Donna used to intrude on this relationship, take over the conversation with her problems. For the future, she feels still in a growth process. Still struggling to "have clearer boundaries," she most longs to be more at peace with herself.

As we learn about who Roberta is to herself, we meet a very different Donna and we begin to understand the complex ways in which these sisters have constructed one another. Roberta, who grew up as her "mother's child," came to experience herself as an empty vessel who existed to fulfill the needs of her mother and sister. Partly the result of her mother's construction of her, Roberta experienced love in symbiotic forms, where she felt most secure as an extension of someone else.

In Roberta's telling, we come to meet a "needy" Donna, incessantly on the verge of some terrible fate that is prevented only by her sister's intervention. Donna's neediness embodies what is meant by a "projective identification" in which Roberta, who is unable to experience her own needs, induces her sister to do the needing for both of them. The result of an intricate, subtle, and largely unconscious process, the drama of need and fulfillment between them maintains fuzzy borders between the sources of need in each of them. Is it Roberta's need to be needed that she sees incessantly enacted in Donna's demands? Or is the (unconscious) pact between them that each will experience all her own (conflictual) needs as originating in the other? It is very striking that Donna did not describe, or even allude to, all the care and ministrations of her from Roberta that seemed central in Roberta's life. Roberta did seem aware of Donna's obliviousness to her efforts when she spoke of needing Donna simply to acknowledge all that Roberta had done for her. In the economy of the unconscious, it is also possible that the "needs" were not primary in Donna but Donna's unconscious provision of the needs Roberta required so that, in gratifying them, Roberta could feel indispensable and not in danger of abandonment. In other words, "I will ask something of you because I know that giving you this opportunity to sacrifice for me is what keeps you from overwhelming anxiety."

Roberta says wistfully that she had given up the wish that Donna acknowledge "all that I went through with her." But Donna sees all that as unwanted (s)mothering and would say that she neither asked for nor wanted all that care. Roberta, of course, attuned to a different level of emotional expression, felt that she was reading accurately Donna's anguish when she wasn't taking care of her. Donna, on her side, would think of this as Roberta's need to see it this way. There is no way of resolving the "reality" of this difference in perception, since the reality exists in their mutual construction of the knot.

One example of this is that Roberta constructs the end of Donna's marriage as her "being abandoned with a baby." Donna saw it as a way of getting along better with Harry and finding a more harmonious way of being parents together. What Roberta saw as a disaster, Donna paints as a positive step toward further growth. Roberta reports that Donna needed a lot of help at this time, but that is not part of Donna's narrative—which, of course, does not mean that Donna was not desperately calling to Roberta for help. There is no vantage point from which we can say how it "really" was. There are only the layers of construction and interaction as these two women engage in a drama of their own creation.

There are unspoken but well-understood rules between Donna and Roberta for how the script of need and fulfillment of need is to be enacted. Donna is to need in a way that Roberta can recognize but Donna can disown. Roberta must give her whatever she needs and Donna is not to notice but must allow her to do this, even if in a martyred fashion. If Roberta tries to get something for herself, Donna must either try to take it away (as Roberta feels she did with her friends) or make Roberta feel guilty—at least, this is how Roberta feels it. From Donna's point of view, to grow apart is to desert Roberta, so she must continually make some place for her—and this may involve staging what Roberta experiences as a calamity that requires her intervention. Neither sister particularly notices that Donna took care of Jennifer for three months while Roberta went in quest of independence. Donna mentions this, but Roberta does not. On the other hand, Roberta feels that rescuing Harry after the collapse of his business (which also kept Will out of jail) was a central event of her twenties, but Donna does not include in her story Roberta's role in this crisis.

Roberta has seen her adult years as a struggle to get out of the quicksand of over-responsiveness to Donna and an effort to develop her own selfhood. While occupationally successful, the most meaningful paths for her have been through relationships—primarily with men. However, it is interesting that Roberta conducted her most passionate love affair, at a time when she thought of Donna as being bereft, in Donna's apartment. Thus, while most separate, she was still connected and she was "having more than Donna" on Donna's turf. And we note that Donna keeps returning to a love relationship with Bert, who was initially Roberta's boyfriend. Donna, too, in being most separate, still carries but disavows her own indelible links to Roberta.

When Roberta is able to ask for and accomplish things in her own interests, she experiences Donna as less in need of her—and she is increasingly able to do this as long as she does not surpass Donna in any way she has to recognize. Getting more than Donna means that she once more has to be very attentive to what Donna may need—or sacrifice what she has in order to restore the equilibrium. She finds Donna's envy destructive and unbearable and must arrange things to maintain what she believes is the unconscious bargain between them—that Donna must never have less than she or, she fears, Donna will abandon her altogether. Thus, warded-off anxieties about abandonment and annihilation pass fluidly between them, each depositing in the other what she can't bear, then guiltily taking it back if the other seems in mortal psychological danger.

Both Donna and Roberta struggle with abandonment fears, separation anxiety, and guilt over dependency as a result of their early deprivation. Their means of internally coping with these painful affects intricately involve the other. Roberta tells me that even as a child, she was unable to allow herself to want anything. Thus, the unconscious bargain with Donna, if it could be expressed in language, might go something like this: you do the needing and wanting and I will hate this in you instead of in me. As Roberta says, she can't stand to be dependent, so she unconsciously arranges for Donna to express this side of her, while Donna remains free to consciously disavow her dependency. Donna accepts this role, while unconsciously directing Roberta to do the clinging (which Roberta disavows) and experience the anxieties and guilt. Dependency, then, is the hot potato these twins pass back and forth, each injecting it into the other.

From early on, in her retrospective account, Roberta experienced Donna's autonomy, initially her success in the world of friends, as an expression of not needing her and, at a deep level, this felt to her like a form of annihilation that was intolerable. Thus, having Donna need her was a way of feeling alive and safe. In her relational space, Donna has found (or created) many people who would, in her words, build her ego and value her talents. Roberta, however, lists no such people. (In fact, it is easy to lose the sense of how competent and creative Roberta is while listening to her relational narrative.) Donna, then, can experience herself as a "free spirit" exploring her capacities in the world but needs to carry with her the guilty, fettered self embodied in Roberta. Roberta can tolerate this as long as she can induce in Donna a need for her care, but she has to abrogate her own successes in the world. Her giving away all of her possessions is the most dramatic example. Donna is free to have a love affair with the world (on behalf of Roberta) while Roberta is charged with maintaining the connections that Donna wishes to disown. From an early time, the twins have created in the other the selves they could not bear to be. The limit to these bargains is that both have to protect themselves and the other from too much envy and its destructive, destabilizing force.

THE WIDER RELATIONAL WEB

We also come to understand, through juxtaposing these stories, that the twins are also, to a large extent, unconsciously enacting their parents' marriage—at least, as they viewed it. Donna had viewed the parental love story as "my father being the *enfant terrible*, while my mother took the strong, martyred position of being right all the time." (Roberta could see the intensity of the love between her parents, but she couldn't understand why her mother stayed with such an irresponsible and frustrating person.) Roberta, as mother's child, is taking the role of their mother vis-à-vis an "irresponsible" father, enacted by Donna, father's child. Roberta reports that their mother had grouped her husband and Donna as the irresponsible ones and sculpted Roberta in her own image as the one to scold, look after, and clean up the messes made by these others who could not be responsible for themselves. Like her mother, Roberta finds herself in a role where she "has to" take care of this "terrible child" even though she ostensibly doesn't want to be doing this. What Donna experiences as her passionate intensity and search for meaning, Roberta sees as recklessness and foolish behavior that she, Roberta, has to rescue her from. On the other side, we suspect that much as the twins' father did not notice all that his wife was doing for him and for the family, Donna doesn't really have to notice Roberta's efforts on her behalf.

With the help of psychotherapy, by age thirty-five, these twins have begun to untangle themselves from one another. It has been difficult, however, to do this and maintain a sense of connection since each is glued to the image they have of the other. Roberta can barely conceive of a Donna who is anything but a needy child. She can barely notice Donna's talents and successes. That is, she may see them, but they are not emotionally important to her. For her part Donna, although she recognizes Roberta's accomplishments, needs Roberta to embody her own helplessness and fear. Thus, these twin sisters have created in the other the shadow sides of themselves and have, throughout their lives, fought against their own creations. And it is rather like shadow boxing, since they each are demanding that the other change the very qualities that she herself has etched into the other.

We might wonder, of course, how these dilemmas will be constructed in the next generation. Donna and Roberta, in different ways, each struggle to experience her child as separate from herself, but we hear the chords of projective processes nevertheless. Alec and Jennifer are still too young for me to interview and write about, but we can look at how the creation of illusion and the creation of the other unfold between parent and child in the two following chapters.

4

No Feelings Allowed on the Stage: Mark and Joan

Mark had not been of much special interest to me until I later interviewed his daughter, Joan, and learned the extent to which their stories are linked. Opaque to one another, they offer narratives that are striking in their reverberations. What I experienced as an almost surreal alignment led me to try to understand their impact on one another. Throughout her life, Joan's psychological world has been shaped by a father who seemed to know how to be, how to live—but who seemed to keep her from being herself. And Mark, on his side, has struggled to discover what being *him*self might mean. Joan has absorbed Mark's internal dilemmas but is unaware that her difficulties in life are his as well.

MARK

When I met Mark, aged fifty-one, a short, thin, balding man with a reserved demeanor, he seemed somewhat dour, but there were sparks of humor. Thinking deeply about himself and his history, he weighed his words, choosing them carefully to be precise. Neither of us knew at the time that I would also interview Joan.

Mark grew up in a small town in Connecticut. On his early map of relationships, Mark places his parents at equal distance from himself but says that he felt great difference in his relationships to each of them. He describes his mother as more available. "I felt safe with her but at the same time I didn't feel so much physical closeness." With his father he felt enjoyable physical connection and warmth. "I would hold his hand and sit on his back and listen to his stories."

He spent most of his days with cousins and age mates who lived nearby. Being small and somewhat weak, however, he was rather inept at sports and often felt inferior to the others. He enjoyed riding horses and collecting flowers, but he never felt part of the main group of children in his nursery school or in his family.

His maternal grandparents were very important to him at this age since they lived in New York and he was frequently taken to stay with them. He recalls, "I was sick and thin, and for some reason I always ate better when I was with my grandmother." Mark's grandfather was a prominent politician who traveled all over the world, and Mark regarded him as a mystical figure. Later, as an adult, he learned that his grandfather kept a mistress in another state and when his grandmother learned of this, she "separated emotionally from him but continued to take care of the house and kids and cater his dinners and events. She stayed involved socially with his life but was emotionally separate. My mother recalled her childhood as lonely, not connected to her father or her mother and my relationship with my mother was influenced by this. There was the same sense of emotional distance where my mother couldn't create an open relationship with her kids." This, of course, is looking back, as Mark tries to trace the roots of what he experienced as a kind of emotional empty space in his relationships. "I never really knew my mother. She was kind of a shadow. She took care of us [here Mark includes his younger siblings], but. . . ."

Mark's father was, like Mark's grandfather, also interested in politics and eventually became mayor of their town. "I experienced my father more emotionally, but his emotion related to his intellectual life. He was similar to my mother's father, interested in politics, traveling, working." Unlike his siblings, Mark learned how to communicate with him on this level, and Mark recalls engaging him in long conversations about history and the historical biographies he liked to read.

Mark's mother was a math teacher. Mark was always a very good student, but he describes himself at age ten as feeling rebellious toward his teachers. Both of his parents were very involved in the life of the school, and Mark didn't dare be anything but a good student.

By this time, Mark had two younger sisters, but he felt different and distant from all of his siblings and didn't feel much connection with them, except for the responsibilities he was given for them by his parents. Once his father became more deeply involved in public life, he was home less and less. His mother became ill with a disease and Mark still wasn't sure what it was, but it left her tired and unable to work or do much in the house. Although he was only ten, many household and child care duties fell to Mark, as the oldest. "I was very proud about this. It became part of the family myth—how much I had done." It fell to Mark to do some of the cooking and cleaning and to watch the younger children. Mark remembers feeling pleased that he was able to be "so grown up" and to fulfill the family expectation to be the responsible, helpful, dutiful child. By this age, Mark had found the place he was scripted to occupy in his family.

At this age, however, Mark still had some opportunity to be boyish, and he tells of a small group of friends with whom he went on trips and shared secrets like "a place in the forest where we built a hut to play in." They enjoyed together a strong fantasy life and he remembers them trying to live out Treasure Island. Mark also found a number of girls to befriend since they were less sports-oriented, and his small size and relative lack of physical coordination continued to keep him on the outskirts of the boys' groups.

When he started middle school, Mark's father was involved in some controversial issues in the town and Mark became aware that many of his friends and their parents were critical of his father. "It was hard for me because I found myself caught between the kids in my class and my father. I didn't like the things they said about him and the jokes they made about him." This was a confusing time for Mark since he still idolized his father and found his classmates' criticisms of him hard to bear.

At age fifteen, as he became much more involved in intellectual life and in the school, eventually becoming head of student government and editing the school newspaper, Mark also began to feel a greater connection with his father. It seemed like he and his father now had even more in common to talk about as they discussed the politics of the school as well as continuing their now more sophisticated discussions of history. As a family, they still sometimes took trips or had outings, but he remembers these largely as an opportunity to go off alone with his father. At this time, he regarded his mother as a kind of unwelcome nag who tried to control his schedule and his whereabouts and he remembers a lot of arguments with her. "But I was still helping a lot in the house, so I figured I could come and go as I pleased, which I did."

As a teenager, Mark also found a new hero in the leader of his church group. "He symbolized for me the romantic personality. He organized campfires and trips and songs. He could do a lot of things, and he knew how to have fun. He was a symbol of what I admired and I wanted to be like him."

Summarizing his experience of adolescence, Mark said, "I was very involved in all these groups but not so much emotionally connected. I was elected to different jobs and took part in different activities, but there was always a certain distance. I felt more connected to the situations than the actual people." Viewing Mark as he now views himself, from some distance, we can see that he continued the pattern of making himself available for what others needed of him—taking responsibility for jobs that needed to be done, offering himself for responsible positions without much feeling about the people who turned to him for leadership and volunteered to follow him.

As he turned twenty, Mark's father became yet more important to him. He really missed him while he was away at college and looked forward to the discussions they would have when he returned home on college vacations. "I didn't share with him too much of what was going on in the other circles of my life, but I loved to talk to my Dad about my ideas. He always wanted to know in great detail what I was studying in all my courses, and I enjoyed telling him."

Feeling shy, Mark had had little involvement with girls at this age, but he continued to make and maintain friendships with other guys, mainly organized around shared intellectual interests, the Debating Society, or going to movies and theater together. In college, he continued to seek and receive various leadership positions and others thought him of as reliable, responsible, and honest. Like his father, Mark majored in history, intent on becoming a teacher, which is what he did.

When Mark was twenty-five, his first girlfriend, Sheila, became pregnant. Sheila had neglected the birth control. They had known each other only four months but decided to marry. "For me it was too early. I was not mature enough to build a family, but at the same time I was mature from age ten so I knew how to take responsibility." Thus, Mark entered marriage out of the same dutifulness with which he took up other roles. With his parents' support, Mark also entered law school in New York. His wife and baby daughter stayed in Connecticut near Mark and Sheila's parents, but Mark commuted, spending weekends at home with his family. In law school, he developed close relationships with his fellow students, again largely based on shared intellectual passions. But he found that he had little in common with old friends from home.

A year later, his second daughter, Joan, was born, but he didn't feel very involved with either of his children. "Mainly my wife was responsible for them—I was very caught up in my studies." He still enjoyed discussing matters with his father, though, who eagerly heard about his new ideas. "I guess I had adopted my father's workaholic style of life," said Mark. After age twenty, Mark's mother and siblings simply drop off his relational map, indicating that they no longer had any psychological or emotional importance to him.

When he was thirty, Mark had returned to his town to practice law. Now it was his wife, Sheila's, turn to live away while seeking more education. All in all, they believed the town to be a terrific place to raise children, and since their parents were nearby and ready to help with the children neither Mark nor Sheila wished to move their home. With Sheila now away part of the week, Mark had to spend more time with his daughters, now three of them—and to get to know them. He described his first child, Gloria, as giving him a lot of trouble with school and home-work. Joan, however, was "not a problem." He felt most connected to Cara, his youngest daughter, since she was still a baby when he took over primary care for them. Later on, though, he began to feel more closeness with Joan because she shared his intellectual interests. He experienced her in much the same way he had his father, a person to spend hours talking about history with, reading the same books and discussing them. Cara, however, reminded him more of his mother and their relationship in-cluded the same kind of tension and strain and overt arguing. Cara was impulsive, emotional, and volatile, and he couldn't understand her.

Reflecting on himself and his life when he was thirty-five and again at forty, Mark focused on his busy practice, his leadership roles in charity or-ganizations, and his teaching at the law school. Again, he had many peo-ple in his life, but not many he felt really close to. There were friends who were "supportive and warm," but no one really special. He hardly men-tions his wife and family during this period except that he experiences their ongoing presence. It was as though he was enacting the role of hus-band and father, doing what was expected of him, but neither his wife nor daughters are drawn other than as outlines, which seems to be how he ex-perienced them. When I asked him specifically to describe them, he was still able to say little about his wife. "We do a good job together," was all he could say about Sheila. Gloria he described as "athletic. She was al-ways out of the house playing some sport or other." Joan was "still the good child, never had any problems, never caused us any problems. Once, I remember, she had some fears, but she got over that." And Cara was the "artistic one—always drawing, kept to herself."

As was his pattern all along, Mark made friends with the people he worked with, people with whom he could share the work stresses and in-tellectual aspects. When an opportunity became available to join an en-counter-type group for lawyers who wanted to improve their interper-sonal skills, when he was forty-eight, Mark signed up, not quite knowing just what he was signing up for. This opened a new world for him. "It was the first time in my life I really had a chance to speak about intimate feel-ings. I'm not sure I even knew what they were before—I never paid much attention to feelings. I was never at all open with anyone. And to do this with other men was extraordinary." He began to take part in a therapy group in New York. "This gave me a chance to be more in contact with myself. I discovered feelings. This group experience changed my life." He spoke about his recognition of the shortcomings of his family of origin. He still felt love for his parents but gradually came to understand that they offered relationships without much real emotional contact. It wasn't until Mark discovered in himself new capacities for feeling that he could see how little space there had been for any kind of feeling in his family of origin—and how much he had kept himself out of the emotional flow of life.

Describing himself at age fifty, just after his father died of a rapid cancer, Mark said that he had become more aware of his father's significance and importance in his life, largely through his psychotherapy. "I miss him terribly in terms of appreciating our connection and in terms of regret that I had not developed with him the connection I could have had. After leaving the mayor's office, he had become a teacher, and I helped him learn about how to be in better contact with his class, how to make better relationships with his students. We also began talking about more personal things and the relationship shifted. I became the more experienced one, the more expert and he came to consult with me."

What Mark had learned about himself at this age was "I have the capacity to be open, to be aware. At the same time, I don't allow myself to do this. Part of this is that I am so busy and part is that there is something in my mentality. My natural state is to remain closed like my mother and father always were. My major difficulty is how to stay really in connection with other people."

Around this time, he was drawn intensely back into his family because of Cara's problems. She was rebellious, taking drugs and failing in school. He was called upon to try to manage things and find help for her. He worried about Cara and couldn't understand what had gone wrong with her. "We didn't know whether to set limits or let her work it out." He had no idea what role he might have played in her difficulties and attributed her behavior to "the times" and "bad friends." Eventually, she had to be hospitalized when she got involved with hard drugs. When I asked him about his relationship with his wife and with his other daughters at this point, he said that he saw his relationship with his wife as being much like the relationship his father had with his mother. They were friends, didn't socialize much with other people, ate together, and talked about the logistics of family life. His older daughters were in college, and not very present for him emotionally. He thought of Joan, particularly, as doing well and succeeding, still causing no one any problem.

Coinciding with these upheavals, which required Mark to give some attention to his emotional state, Mark had a relationship with another woman, Elyse, "who I felt I really could communicate with at a deeper level. I could tell her my feelings and it was exciting, like flying free. But I felt loyal to my wife and family. I had a strong sense of commitment and security and I didn't want to rock the boat." Eventually, his wife discovered his affair and insisted that he break it off as a condition of her staying with him. "After that, she felt less secure, had lots of anger, but she still has love and care and wants to be with me." Mark speaks of this without much emotion, but there is just a hint of regret for where "flying free" might have taken him.

At the time of our meeting, Mark was now president of the local bar association organization and focused on his work and many roles. His professional prominence brought with it many relationships, but still Mark often continued to "feel aloof, as though I don't really belong anywhere. But I'm working on it."

He regretted that he had so much difficulty developing closeness within his family. "I didn't allow myself to be more direct with my family, didn't develop special relationships with my children. But I'm still trying to change that. And I'm also trying to deepen my friendships. I guess I always felt that, like at age ten, I had to be the responsible, grown-up one. I had to be strong for everyone."

Mark's assessment of his relational biography seems pretty astute. He recognizes the way in which he has been in relationships without really being "in" them, being what others expect him to be, developing connection at an emotional distance. That Mark fulfills others' behavioral expectations of him so well has kept people with him, and it seems that, except for Elyse and his therapy group, no one has been able to penetrate the shell behind which Mark enclosed himself. Mark, through therapy, came to understand that his closing himself off was part of a family pattern that traced back to his grandparents' marriage, through his mother's emotional distance. Mark only remembers being emotionally enlivened by men whom he could admire and aspire to be like—his father and his church counselor. These were the only figures he could imbue with feeling and construct as people of emotional significance to him. The women in his life were largely taken in as people to please, to do for, but not to make meaningful, except to the extent that his third daughter, Cara, caused family problems (to be solved) or his second daughter, Joan, reminded him of his father and engaged him intellectually.

JOAN

It was to learn about how Joan might have experienced Mark as a father that I sought permission to interview her. Mark seemed to have cast Joan as like his father and, therefore, like himself, and I wondered about whether he had, in fact, in some way, created her in this mold.

I met Joan when she was twenty-five. A slim, attractive young woman with long red hair, she was eager to talk and struggled to put her feelings into words. Joan described herself as having grown up in "a close family," the middle of three sisters who were a year apart in age. She remembers age five as a very happy time in which she felt surrounded by her mother, father, and grandmother. Joan's mother put a lot of energy into entertaining the children, taking them to plays and movies, reading them stories, involving them in projects and games. By contrast, Joan described her father as largely absent. He was very busy, rushing from one job and responsibility to the next, with little time to be with his children. Her maternal grandmother, who lived nearby, always seemed happy when Joan and her sisters came over to spend time with her. "She gave us a lot of attention and warmth. It was good to be at her place—quiet and relaxed."

Joan felt that she and her sisters grew up as a group and were treated as a group. Joan, looking back, felt that she needed most to have her parents' interest and affection. "I seemed to be more interested in being close to both my parents and finding ways in which I could get their attention and find things of common interest with them. I tried to be like them so I could find common things. They always used to say I was the good girl who never gave them any trouble. I was the pleaser—they were satisfied with me." At this point, we hear the reverberation of Mark's words—the child who "never gave any trouble."

Joan felt very competitive with her sisters for her parents' love but was not close to them. Even as young as age five, she had her own friends whom she preferred to play with. Trying as hard as she could to ignore her sisters and pretend that they were not there, Joan tried to be a leader among her friends and organize activities with and for them. She thinks of herself at around this age as trying to be like an adult; she would try to be the helper of the kindergarten teacher and the one among the class who could be relied upon to be responsible.

Growing up in a small town with the extended family nearby, there were always grandparents, aunts, uncles, and cousins available to be with when her parents were busy. There were many homes where she could enter and watch TV, stay for dinner, play, or just spend time. Joan felt welcomed and free to roam. When her parents were busy or out of town, it was an easy move to stay with other relatives or with her friends' families.

Drawing her life at age ten, Joan featured a "boyfriend" who had become important to her at age eight. He was from her class at school and "we considered ourselves like a couple, really good friends. We even thought we would get married, like a dream. We really felt we were in love." Here, Joan remarks that she sees the beginning of a pattern of hers, to commit herself to someone and then to cool off. "It's a pattern of mine to have dreams, have a perfect ideal—and then it doesn't—things change. We kept on being together. But then I didn't feel we had enough in common after awhile. Something inside of me has always been looking for an ideal partner." Joan remembers her longing at this age to be part of the adult world and having a boy to be with in a special way made her feel grown up, like her parents, having someone all to herself.

Going to school in this small community, she felt very much a part of her class. But it was hard to feel close to any specific person when there was so much of a group feeling. She had lots of activities with her group, including Girl Scouts and church and extracurricular classes as well as trips and outings on weekends. Of this semi-rural, small town environment, Joan said, "I always felt it was an ideal setting, thought it was wonderful to be with friends doing interesting things together. When we were together, it would be a warm feeling of togetherness, but there wasn't the distinction of talking about personal things, like about my relations with my family. It wouldn't seem appropriate to share feelings with them."

Around this time, age ten, Joan began to sense some reserve in herself toward her family. She felt that it didn't come freely to her to express affection. She had a sense of wanting to be close to her parents but felt it was hard for all of them to really let themselves experience the closeness. "I was closer to the kids my age. That took a lot of my attention. My family got to be farther in focus. Usually my parents were very busy and into other things and I didn't really feel their presence with me. I guess I just gave up, didn't feel it was possible any more. I was aware of the gap between how I would have wanted the relationship to be and how it was. I felt that there was some kind of distance between me and them. If I tried to talk to my mother, she wasn't really with me. She was spacing out. With my father, we would usually talk about intellectual things and I also felt that he is not really aware of what is happening to me in other parts of my life. I tried to be accepted by him, did things to be closer to him. I looked up to him, idolized him really. He was smart and seemed to know everything, could fix everything. And I was the strong one that he could count on. My parents were very proud of me. They weren't aware of my difficulties. They didn't really know me." Even her grandmother was by now at a greater distance. "She was better for younger children. As we grew older, she had a hard time relating to us. I wasn't drawn to her so much any more." We note here that, as for Mark, being strong, not giving anyone trouble, and hiding one's inner self are all interrelated and amount to much the same thing.

With her extended family, Joan was also feeling more hesitant and distant. "I didn't feel as comfortable to go to their houses. I was more self-conscious and shy, felt maybe I wasn't so accepted there—like not being so sure if they liked me or not—if they really want me there."

Even by age ten, Joan had a strong sense of how she was expected to be and felt unable to "express fears or the dark things about me. I always felt I had to be strong and appropriate and there were sides I couldn't show. I couldn't act silly—I was very serious." Once, Joan remembers trying to tell her father how afraid she was of the dark and all the rituals she developed to try to soothe herself and be able to fall asleep. Often she couldn't sleep until daybreak because she was so terrified. Her father just told her this was silly, that there was nothing to be afraid of, and she never spoke of it again.

Looking back, even at age ten, then, Joan thinks she sensed that something was missing in her family. The structure was there, everyone was enacting a family, but she felt the absence of something she couldn't name. She remembers her dog at this age, and telling him her feelings. "He was really more my dog than anyone else's and I almost felt like he could really understand me. I never had a diary. I had my dog."

In the midst of her adolescence at age fifteen, Joan found herself increasingly critical of her mother. She felt that her mother was too different, too spontaneous. She wanted her to care more about what people thought, as Joan did, and not dress in unusual outfits or act so much like a teenager herself. "My mother just seemed to live in her own world. I wanted her to fit in and be like other people. I wished she was more aware of me and my life." Joan had tried to be close to her older sister, but their competition got in the way. She felt vulnerable, and she felt that her sister criticized her and put her down.

For the first time, Joan began having trouble with her schoolwork. The math had gotten beyond her and she feared to let anyone know. When she could no longer hide her failing grades, she confided in her father who was, she was glad to find, supportive of her. "For the first time, I felt that I could express my weaknesses a little bit. I felt I could be accepted even though I have all those faults." Joan's father arranged for her to have a math tutor, and she was able to resume being the "good student" of the family. Sometimes, too, her father tried to cheer her up by taking her to a museum or a movie. He still felt like the strong person she could admire and rely on, someone worth trying to be strong for.

Joan felt that she really needed to grow up through her friends, and she describes a large number of them, regarding them primarily along an axis of how much of herself she felt she could express with each. Joan was closest during this time to two boys. With Ned, three years older and in another state, she felt safe to confide some of her estrangement from her family. They also created a safe and passionate relationship together, mostly in letters. They enjoyed fantasizing about the relationship they were having, agonizing about missing each other although they saw each other only rarely. Joan could talk to him because he was an outsider and far enough away that she could share more of herself.

Joan's other close friend was Ralph, with whom she had her first sexual relationship. They had fun together, but the relationship was mostly physical. He was from a lower social class and adored her. It was nice to be with him because he completely accepted her and she was able to feel free and comfortable, but she never felt he could understand her so she never tried to bring the more confusing parts of herself to the relationship.

By age twenty, off at Rutgers, Joan found herself part of several different groups of friends. She had joined a group house with some of the people she had grown up with, trying to make a safe environment with lots of sharing in the shadow of a large impersonal state university. Again, Joan emerged a leader but didn't feel particularly close to anyone. She was responsible, looked to as someone who could arrange things and take care of things but then feared to show her "darker" side to anyone. And it is significant that Joan labels the hidden aspects of herself her "dark" side—she was a child who was afraid of the "dark."

She was able to find some closeness with Mel who seemed patient enough to try to know her. She felt able to open up to him some, but he finally left the group house and went in search of himself elsewhere. Joan then turned to Larry although she didn't feel as comfortable with him. Larry "wasn't open himself. He had a hard time expressing feelings and really talking about things. But I felt that he was interested in me and wanted to be close and really put energy into maintaining the relationship."

Although away at college, Joan worked hard to maintain contact with the people she grew up with. "We really had to work to keep these relationships going. There was this deep feeling of connection with the people at home because we grew up together and had been through everything together, so there was a feeling of commitment. I had a strong feeling of being connected to a group and having closer people around me when I went home. Being with these old friends met a strong social need even though I couldn't talk to them about my new experiences or what I had been feeling." Joan continues to categorize her relationships in terms of how much of herself they seem to allow her to express—and to others' capacities to be open themselves.

When she was home for vacations, Joan tried again to be closer to her father. "I still looked up to him and gave him a lot of credit for his work. My own interests in political science were close to his interests in law, so we had many things in common. I tried to include him in my life in many things and get closer to him. It worked, sort of, but I always felt frustrated that we weren't close enough. He was interested but still very busy with what he was doing so he couldn't really be there when I needed him. I had a hard time really expressing myself with him. I felt that it was really important to me for him to know me, but it just never worked out."

Joan, on the other hand, sensed her mother as trying to be closer to her but felt that her mother "didn't really know how to relate to me. She didn't feel comfortable next to me. She was into herself with the different problems she had, couldn't really come out of herself. She seemed not to be so much in touch with reality. She was always very idealistic and she didn't see problems. She would be shocked and get really depressed if anyone's life didn't go according to plan."

Joan had always sensed that her parents weren't really interested in one another and she saw their relationship as a model for what she did not want in her own life. "They'd talk about logistical things, but I never saw any affection between them."

By age twenty-five, Joan's main focus in her life was to try to develop more personal relationships with people. She was working in a government job as a political aide but was trying hard to develop herself as a person. "I do my job well, but what really counts is figuring out who I am."

She had begun living with Henry, who had been most important in helping her learn to come out of the shell she felt had imprisoned her. "He was very different from my father, very easygoing, more spontaneous, not as intellectual or serious. I felt I could really feel free with him and express myself pretty much even though I always had a sense of wanting the relationship to be more than what it was. I wanted him to be more interested in my inner life. There was a good feeling of closeness but it wasn't put in words. Many times I'd think we weren't close because it wasn't put in words but other times I'd look at it and see the feeling was there. But my expectations were such that I wasn't satisfied—I also was very confused about making a commitment or not. Even though the relationship was not everything I wanted it to be, I had a strong need to be together a lot. I was afraid of being alone."

The time for decision making came when Henry was offered a job in another city and Joan decided not to go with him. "It's a close relationship. I am no longer afraid of being alone. It works well for me to know that he's there and to meet once in a long while but not be together all the time."

Joan had found that at this age she has begun to accept her mother more and to see good qualities in her. She continued to idealize her father and think of him as someone who had everything figured out. "He was so knowledgeable and successful, but I could never imagine talking to him about how I felt about anything. We discussed ideas, he was interested in my work, but the conversation was never personal."

For the first time, Joan has found it possible to have emotionally close relationships with women friends. Until recently, she had always sensed that other women kind of envied her—her looks, her success, her easy friendships with men. She has joined a New Age Buddhist group and has found a few friends with whom she can share feelings and experiences. She continues to struggle with her tendency to hold herself back and feel unfree in the relationship, fearing to express herself emotionally.

As Joan became clearer on her experience of distance from others, she found that her younger sister, Cara, felt the same way as she. This discovery of conflict in common brought them together and they began to explore the similarities in their personalities and early histories. This shared inner search has brought them together for the first time in their lives and she now regards Cara as her best friend. "In recent years, she has become about the only person I can really talk to freely. She had had a lot of problems growing up, but I now see that we have a lot in common."

Together, she and Cara have begun to approach their father to talk about how they have all come to feel so far from each other emotionally. "We started talking about very personal things including our relationship and what has happened through the years. I started seeing him more as an equal, stopped looking up to him, and we became friends. I started seeing many things in our personalities that are similar. I realize now that I never really knew him."

All the other friends and people in her life Joan discusses in terms of how well they know her and how much of herself she can express with them. Nell, a woman she works closely with, is important because "I feel very open and natural—can be myself without a need to judge myself for things. She accepts me and that helps me really accept myself as I am." She continues to feel frustrated in her distant relationship with her older sister. "I really wish I could make her understand how I see things, but we don't see each other very much."

With Marty, a friend from her work world, "I can share with him things that happen to me—things I'm concerned with and things he's concerned with in his family. I used to have fantasies about him but now we know it's a brother/sister relationship."

With Don, her occasional lover, "It's a very open kind of relationship. I can express my feelings. We get into a lot of arguments and can get closer from it. We can feel close physically, we just share things together." With Ben, a friend from her Buddhist group, "I feel close to him spiritually. We just feel that we know each other—really clearly like we can really see each other and talk about things that touch us deeply."

At age twenty-six, then, Joan is intensely involved in trying to bring her real self to her relationships with others to be seen and recognized, to take the risk of revealing herself and being known. Growing up in what appears to have been a relational environment of security and attachment, Joan purchased a "special" place in the family at the price of becoming a "pleaser" as she put it. She learned to be an exceptionally good girl, burying all that might not be so acceptable and lovable in herself. In her eagerness to be other than part of a group of sisters, Joan hurried herself to be "grown-up" and join her parents. To do this, she had to disavow her silliness and immaturity, all the feelings that are natural to a child, to which a child is entitled. However, early on she began to sense that she had left an important part of herself behind and began to struggle with when and if she dared risk her success as an admired leader and exemplary daughter and student by exposing what she felt to be the "darker" parts of herself. Since then, Joan has begun connecting to others based on the degree to which she feels that they are people who can accept and respond to the more emotional and thus more vulnerable and "real" parts of herself, and she is quite consciously aware of this. She intensely needs people to validate her inner experiences rather than just expect her to do what she is supposed to do. She needs people who will mirror and hear her rather than "spacing out" as she felt her mother did. However ambivalently, she wants people to "know" her.

Like many other people, especially many young people, Joan's focus on others is seeing herself in their eyes, hoping to find in their acceptance of her a path to acceptance of herself. Easily finding a place in a group, feeling part of a group, Joan hopes to see in others the secret of her own uniqueness but fears being too unique, too different. The problem, then, of being for others versus being herself with others dominates Joan's odyssey of connection to others.

REPEATING HISTORY

These are two highly competent, successful people but they each feel imprisoned behind a wall of petrified emotions. In many ways, Joan's history repeats Mark's. Both are in search of personal expressiveness, relationships in which they can be open, speak their hearts, and feel free with others, and both feel closed and frightened of disclosing themselves. While they are at present groping toward each other, delicately trying to find openings for what they would each experience as intimate conversation, there is something tragic in this story of two people reaching for each other and not quite touching. To both Mark and Joan, it feels as though other people won't allow them to express their feelings in the raw form that feels like true expression. Both feel that others require that they stay controlled, in charge of themselves, confident, and without weakness or vulnerability. What remains "dark" are the chaotic anxieties that attend intense affect and inner reality.

While Joan was growing up, particularly as a teenager, Mark saw her as being like himself in her intellectual focus, drive, and capacity for leadership. He describes her as "never being any trouble," but although he sees much of himself in her, he never imagines that she may struggle with the same sense of being silenced and closed off that he has. Rather, she seems to him like his best self without any of the longing or loneliness—this is his illusion of her. Beyond that, he doesn't really notice her.

The story of the nighttime fears, although a small one in their narratives, because they each tell it, might give us a clue to the processes by which they may have mutually constituted one another. Joan, terrified of the dark, breaks out of the well-controlled, "good girl with no problems" script she has lived out for her father and tells him of her fears. Mark responds (in Joan's telling) by scoffing at her and (in his telling) making them go away. If we might imagine a close-up focus on this one interaction as a metaphor for their relationship, we see Mark insisting that she maintain herself as though without anxieties, which signify inner life (that he is unable to bear in himself), and he offers her his own style of ignoring or overcoming, or at least suppressing, whatever might be upsetting. Joan, on her part, tries to take in her father's cool rationality, which strengthens her idealization of his ability to manage all things but also tells her that feelings are not to be privileged or expressed. Mark manages her terror much as he does his own, thus offering a behavioral example of how he may have unwittingly created in her the same internal constellation and, at the same time, confirmed her illusion of him as strong enough to vanquish even the demons of the night.

As he has gotten older and explored his life in therapy, Mark has come to better understand his own role in the emotional distance he creates in relationships. He has found in himself the closed door, but that doesn't mean he can easily open it. It is still too easy to fall into old patterns of socially expected joviality, which makes him a sought-after companion for others but leaves him feeling like he is playing a part and not fully participating in the relationship. And, at midlife, intimacy seems more important to Mark than anything else.

With Elyse, Mark was able to experience himself as emotionally open. He could tell her all his thoughts and feelings and was somewhat dizzied by the experience. But, as he tells it, the calls of duty and family pulled him back. We might, of course, wonder if his own ambivalence about this aspect of himself wasn't a larger factor in his leaving Elyse. To change so much at midlife is to risk not quite knowing who one is.

Both Mark and Joan are in some ways muscle-bound by their own competence. They had both been admired, respected, and liked by others for their intelligence, their success, and their leadership qualities and both had in some ways become afraid to put all this at risk. Both feared that they had to be what others valued in them and that to show another side of themselves meant sacrificing what they had earned. For such people, feelings that don't fit their image often go underground and are barely visible even to themselves. Mark and Joan felt rather like imposters who can bring only part of themselves to their lives.

Joan has come to the realization of what she needs in relationships much earlier in her development than did her father. It still feels to her like she needs only to find the right person and she will be able to be the open, expressive person she wishes to be. Again and again, she believes that she has found such a person, only to become disappointed in them and renew the search. She fears what she calls her "darker side." Because she can't accept these feelings, whatever they may be, in herself, she worries that no one else will be able to either. Thus she withholds this part of herself, which only convinces her that she cannot find a place for it in her relationships. Like her father, she is successful in her life, but only partly present. She allows others to construct her as completely "together," an attractive, ambitious young woman who knows where she is going and how to get there. Others envy her, unaware of the turmoil within her. Her public persona, then, seems to be much like Mark's.

Throughout her life, Joan regarded her father as a hero, kept him on a pedestal, as someone to emulate, but someone too far away from her to really be close to. She engaged him by sharing ideas on topics that interested him; this made for conversation and connection between them. Only in her mid-twenties has Joan begun to recognize his more human and personal qualities—"I never really knew him," she says, just as Mark describes his own father. She seems to both know and not know that he suffers from the same sense of emotional frozenness that she has. In response to his effort to be more emotionally available, as a result of his therapy (which she doesn't seem to know about), she has begun to talk more openly with him. With this window in their relationship, she wants to get to know him, but at the same time she is reluctant to sacrifice her notion of the idealized, always rational, father who is so central to her own sense of self. She wants her father to know the vulnerability in her; she is less prepared to accept the vulnerability in him.

Feeling that she is "like" her father, as she pictures him, gives Joan a source of strength, but it also binds her to being contained. The culture of characters with whom she has, by choice, filled her life stage all serve as people who seem to either open her or close her down. Joan is still uncertain about just which characters she wants to keep in her life: she somewhat fears those who invite her to be open—or at least, quickly finds fault with them. At the same time, she disdains those who reflect the closed-up part of herself. We therefore can imagine Joan as having a relational script at the ready—a script that auditions others for the part of helping her to express herself. She is still casting the actors, trying to find someone she can unconsciously create as a suitable container for the deeper and more chaotic aspects of her internal struggle.

We can see relatively clearly how Mark-as-he-seemed-to-be-for-Joan had a lasting imprint on her emotional life. It is more difficult to ask what sort of character Joan has been for Mark. Part of Mark's orientation to the world is that he doesn't really notice people for their qualities and keeps himself at such an emotional distance that he doesn't seem to need much of them except for the quiet security of their presence and their role in creating a structure for his life. Thus, we hear little from him about his wife except that she is "loving" in a distant sort of way. Joan describes her flamboyance; Mark does not. Mark and his wife have been successful partners in their project of raising children together, sharing child care and the responsibilities. We hear from both Mark and Joan that Sheila has been intensely involved in her own interests, but she remains a shadowy character for both of them. Mark has structured himself so as to need little from others except sharing of intellectual interests. Only recently has he been able to formulate for himself the emotional, more personal connection that has been missing all his life—and to have the courage to try to repair this. Without realizing it, he has responded to Joan in such a way as to create in her the same distrust of emotional experience that he developed in his own family.

Mark tends to respond emotionally to people only when they make waves or cause him trouble. Joan was not such a child—she "never caused me any problems." As long as Joan seemed to be unproblematically going about her life, he didn't focus much on who she was or who she was becoming. That she was out of the house so much, involved in activities with her various groups of friends, seemed to him normal and expectable. In some ways, he didn't foresee having much of a relationship with her beyond his responsibilities to her as a provider and caretaker. That she shared some of his interests in history and politics was a nice bonus, but not one to provoke intense emotions in him. Joan says that he was proud of her, but Mark doesn't say so. To feel proud of someone means to experience part of oneself in them, to have a sense that one has something to do with encouraging or nurturing that person in such a way that it has led to success or triumph. Mark, who has felt so closed off from himself, does not experience himself in others. Mark seemed rather to assume that Joan was much like him—intellectual, focused, without much inner life or many strong feelings. In effect, he understood her to be the self he proclaimed himself to be for the world, and it never seems to have occurred to him that Joan struggled with the same conflicts about how to make one's inner life part of one's outer reality. Perhaps Mark hoped to create in Joan an untroubled version of the self he wished to be.

For Joan, Mark has enacted the good father but without emotional presence. Joan has sensed this but has, until recently, been unable to put this experience into words. There is no complaint she can lodge against him; to the contrary, she sees all his good qualities. But there is an emotional absence for which there is no name. The missing quality is one that would offer a kind of emotional freedom through emotional resonance and responsiveness, something that Joan perhaps remembers from some very early experiences of childhood when she could just be all of herself without censoring or suppressing. This is something Joan needs and wants but is uncertain how to look for—or to even know if she has found it.

In some sense, both Mark and Joan "need" the other to embody the well-organized, efficient, intellectual selves that they each try both to be and not to be, at the same time. Neither is comfortable with inner chaos, the rattles of ambivalence and irrationality that threaten to upend their smooth outer functioning. Each feels they have to "be" the reliable, sensible one for the other because this, in a paradoxical way, allows them awareness of their inner states. If someone outside seems to have unassailable rationality and good sense, then one can at least allow oneself one's own flights of fancy and emotion, however privately or shamefully. Mark always felt he had to be strong for his children; Joan felt she had to be strong for her father. Thus, constructing the other as "the strong one" both allows each a sense of security and inner freedom at the same time that it traps each in their shell.

It may be that, in this family, Cara has been the one chosen, by Mark and Joan at least, to live out the uncontrolled feelings that each fears in himself or herself. Cara expresses herself—artistically, emotionally, sexually, and with substance abuse. Neither Mark nor Joan could really understand her, since she was a foil to their contained, responsible selves. She serves to remind them of the psychological dangers of letting down one's guard and may indeed contain, through the processes we have been considering, pieces of their own irrational and chaotic selves. It is of interest that the more comfortable Joan grows with her own confusing emotions and vulnerabilities, the closer she allows herself to be to Cara—as though she is taking back some of what she (and Mark) had disowned and deposited into her sister.

With Mark and Joan, we can witness the emotional construction of self that exists beyond identification. At one level, one could say that Joan simply imitates or models her father, and this analysis has some truth in it. However, it does not explain why Joan has the same internal struggles and longings as her father when she is, at least consciously, blind to this aspect of him. Joan has become the way she is in large part because it was the only way she could get her father to really "see" her. One's sense of place in the world depends to a large extent on one's sense of the place one has been given by others in growing up.

The danger in not fulfilling the roles that a person as important as her father assigns to her is that she risks not being seen by him at all. The fear of disappearing for another, of no longer existing for them, is a profound terror. It is better to be a partial self or a false self than not to have meaning for the other at all. For Joan, then, it is completely understandable that she tests new people she meets to discover what aspects of her they will be able to tolerate seeing. We can imagine that inside she wonders, Can you see my vulnerability and fears or are you, like my father, simply going to be blind to what else I am besides the responsible, good girl? Joan's development therefore is poised on this issue. And with this example, we can see the way in which a child's life can be deeply affected by the unsolved unconscious problems of his or her parent through the mechanisms of "being" for that parent some aspect of their own inner world.

There is yet another explanation to consider about the link between Mark and Joan. Notably, shortly after Joan began to attend closely to her emotional distance in relationships and to strive to express more of herself, Mark began his own odyssey of doing the same. As far as I know from these interviews, they didn't speak about these things with one another, yet the coincidence is striking. One function of (unconsciously) relocating one's own difficulties in another person is in hopes that that person will manage them better and one can then reinternalize the more organized and less dread-filled emotional solutions. We can't, of course, say with certainty that this is what happened for Mark, that Joan unconsciously transmitted her more managed, less anxiety-filled state in regard to self-expression, but such an interpretation at least serves to illustrate one of the functions of creating one's own conflicts in another—the possibility of repair. This is what good mothers of infancy and psychotherapists strive to do. The therapist, on the receiving end of the patient's unmanageable conflicts, processes them through her or his own resources and, in the best case scenario, offers it back in less toxic form (Bion, 1962; Ogden, 1982). When such a process is successful, the person can take back the part of his psyche now transformed into bearable, thinkable form. Thus, Mark becomes able to talk about his effort to be more open about and aware of his inner life which, before, he just automatically fled. If, indeed, Joan "contains" Mark's conflicts over expression of the inner self, then her persistent striving to manage her fears of this may be a way of mending Mark's damaged self as well. In this sense, she doesn't bat away his fears (as he did hers) but, through internalizing them and organizing them in a way that is less threatening and overwhelming, offers them back in more manageable form. As she confronts her terrors of empty solitude, she assuages his, all without having to speak about it. Viewed this way, Mark and Joan may now be unconsciously aiding the other in overcoming their dread of bringing themselves into emotional engagement with the world.

The conversations that Mark and Joan have recently begun have engendered for each of them an opportunity to test their illusions of the other and to expand their vision. In this manner they move toward finding rather than creating each other, and this opens new vistas of growth for each of them, not only in how they view the other but what becomes possible to express in themselves.

5

"A Daughter Is a Daughter": Mary and Lavinia

"Children," writes Carolyn Steedman, "are always episodes in someone else's narrative" (1986, 122). When I had asked Mary why she had Lavinia—or any of her children—she just shrugged and said, "It's just what you did." Mary was therefore not aware of any particular hopes or aspirations for Lavinia—or anything she wanted her to fulfill for her. But Lavinia, like all children, was born into an ongoing drama, a drama in which she was to find—and be assigned—a place. And she, for her part, constructed a new narrative, one that made sense of the people that preexisted her in her family.

MARY

Mary, a fifty-five-year-old woman, was living a rural life in southern Michigan. She looked much like a stereotype would predict—attractive in a matronly sort of way. A somewhat reticent woman, she showed flashes of great warmth and, although talking to a psychologist seemed rather strange to her, she was curious about what it would be like and was very open in telling me her relational history.

Mary grew up on a farm in southern Michigan, not far from where she had lived all her adult life. Her autistic brother who claimed much of her mother's attention dominated her early childhood. "I remember being off to the side and people doing for him a lot. He had to be tied into a chair and fed." Two other siblings were born when she was a teenager, but Mary said she feels as though she had been an only child. It was her mother's brother, her uncle Richard, and his wife, her aunt Grace, whom she remembers fondly as people who made "a fuss" over her and would come to take her places. Of her parents, Mary said, "I knew they loved me and I felt cared for, but they were busy with what they had to do. My mother was sick when I was growing up—she had heart problems and I remember waiting for her to move her head during her afternoon nap—just so I could talk to her."

I asked Mary how she experienced love as a child and she spoke of her father who would pick her up and play with her. Her mother would occasionally tell her stories at bedtime. "I felt a part of the whole thing, but that was also because of the extended family members involved. I was the only grandchild. My aunt and uncle never had children, so all the aunts and uncles made some fuss over me. My mother was never bad to me, but she had moved from the town to the country to be a farmer's wife. She loved to read. With more opportunity, she would have been an intellectual. But at age five, I felt like the child of all of them, with no special caretaker."

Mary never formed a relationship with her brother Claude. He was barely functional and eventually, when Mary was nine, the family had to put him in an institution.

When she was ten, with her brother gone, she felt more attention from her parents. Her father would work with her in the garden, "he would take me with him when he went to deliver cherries to the canning factory. He didn't spend much time with me on a daily basis, but when he did it was unique and wonderful. I would ride on the tractor and he made me feel that I was his kid and I was great." Her face lights up when she speaks of her father. He was also the disciplinarian, but Mary thought he was always fair. "He would paddle us, but then come up and talk to me so I knew I was reinstated."

Mary also enjoyed time with her grandfather, who "could do many things and I tootled around the farm with him—I'd sit on his lap, he'd tell me stories—we'd play talent show and he'd clap—he was very entertaining." She had an aunt Ruby who was "like a big sister, just seventeen herself. She'd play hide and seek, we'd do kid-type things. Then she was killed in a freak accident when I was eleven. She is the person I would lay in bed and talk to and cry to. I did this even after she died." With her mother, though, Mary felt an emotional distance. "She saw that I had clothes and fed me, but there was not that interaction that I have with my girls—she was in the kitchen doing her work." And still there were her aunt Grace and uncle Richard to take her places, get her the things she wanted, and give her "extra spoiling." At this age, Mary remembers being a part of a group of girls at her church, but no one really stands out or felt very close.

Mary's memory of her childhood, then, has as dramatis personae a loving extended family, a distant mother, and her father as its sparkling, emotionally dominant center. The girl/woman whom she could be close to, in play and in sharing herself, was lost to her.

When she was fifteen, her younger sister, Wendy, was born and felt to her like a live doll to take care of while her mother did chores. Around this time her grandmother died. The family went through a very rough year two years later when her mother's heart problems became more serious. It was her father who took her to the city to buy clothes—"He even took me to get my first bra"—and her mother, somewhat enviously, used to comment on the special relationship she had with him. Her mother told her that she was able to get her father to do things for her that he would not do for anyone else, and Mary relished how special she was to him.

Mary described her mother as having been a people-collector, someone always willing to take in people who needed a place to stay—down and out relatives or even people she hardly knew who were recovering from some sort of personal tragedy in their lives. Her mother would invite these people to live in their home and would care for them. Mary thought that this was her mother's way of enlarging her world, but still Mary felt that it reflected some kind of lack in herself. "I guess we weren't interesting enough for her," Mary said. Although Mary described herself as feeling "secure" in her extended family, she wanted also to feel that she could be special and interesting to someone and this she succeeded in mainly with her father.

As a teenager, Mary began trying harder to be in touch with others of her own age, despite the difficulty of living in such an isolated place. She met Helen in a youth group and found a similarity: "We identified with each other—farm backgrounds, intellectual mothers and good farm men fathers—we sort of clicked. She always had good advice for me." Finally, she had someone besides her much-missed aunt, someone present, to share her experiences with. Her first effort at dating was fairly disastrous, however. She hesitated to put Andrew on her map. "He dated me a couple of times then dated someone else—I was devastated." She had been infatuated with Andrew and when he stopped dating her, she concluded, painfully, that she must be unattractive and undesirable.

When she was eighteen, while working as a counselor at a church summer camp, one of her friend's brothers "took a liking to me and gave me self-confidence when I went into college that fall." She barely remembers this young man, but she remembers how his attention to her gave her hope that she could be attractive to men. Still, it was another nice surprise when, while at college, "another boy picked me over one of my friends." Through these experiences with men she barely remembers, Mary was beginning to feel like a woman with men.

More surprises were in store when Andrew, the boy who had first rejected her, again showed an interest in her when she was nineteen. They became engaged a year later. "There was a certain chemistry we always had. I was unhappy with college. I had dated a couple others, and . . . I was real comfortable with him—his mother and I were friends—she seemed to really like me. Growing up in this community, getting married was important. You didn't want to blow it and not get married at all."

Mary's engagement initiated the first closeness to her mother she mentioned. "We would talk about planning the wedding and all that—it was the first time we could talk 'girl talk.'"

Andrew was six years older than Mary. "We had good physical chemistry. But he has a sense of taking charge, knowing more, correcting my speech, criticizing me. He fit into my family, which is more casual. His family is more critical. He had three sisters who were born baking and cooking and they criticized me for not baking rolls, and made me feel inadequate or that I couldn't live up to it. He thought I was a farm girl with all that he thought it meant, but I wasn't. I liked music and books and other things." After they married, Mary and Andrew moved to his farming community. "It was culture shock even though we grew up just fifteen miles away from one another. His county is much more judgmental—people couldn't be different there. He had an enormous family with twelve children. The men would eat first and then the women. I was shocked by their very chauvinistic attitudes." Her father visited frequently to help the young couple with their new home and seemed proud of her. Mary, who took a secretarial job in the local church, organized her life around the church and committee work. "I had contacts with people but they weren't really influential for me. I did a lot of reading."

Between ages twenty and twenty-five, she met Esther through her church work and they worked alongside one another. "She was a mentor, I could go to her. She had good attitudes about people; she helped me understand my husband better because she knew his family background. She thought the best of people and looked on the good side. She always found value somewhere, admitting that not everyone is perfect. These were values I wanted to adopt." Esther thus occupied the place of woman counselor, someone Mary needed to have in her life.

Mary's mother seemed still to be too busy with her life to have much space for Mary. They fought over her mother's "arrogance" about how Mary's home should be decorated. "She meant well, but it created fights because I felt insulted by her implying that I wouldn't know how to do it. She wasn't overpowering, but subtle and helpful and that made it harder—she wanted to give us things, but my husband hated it."

With respect to the few friends she had had from high school and college, Mary felt inferior. They were getting into professions while she had returned to the farm. "For fifteen years I tried to please him. I realized after a while that I wasn't myself anymore. I was happy about him and the kids and the farm and our sex life, but I wasn't happy about myself. The adjustments I was making weren't making him happier."

By the time she was twenty-five, Mary had given birth to a son and a daughter. She hadn't felt ready for the first pregnancy, but adapted. Andrew "left early in the morning, came late at night. It was a solid, but volatile relationship. We have a power struggle—neither of us wants to be put down. We'd have discussions where I'd cry for three hours. He needs to have somebody to control. We fought about disciplining the children. He believed in do as I tell you and I believed in explaining. He loves me dearly, but I've wondered if the choice ever came between his mother, me, and farming—I don't know—he's very much a family man." How did you experience his love for you? I asked Mary. "Sexually, verbally. He'd do things for you—bring home lilacs from the yard, bring home ice cream. And yet, to hear him talk to you sometimes, you'd feel totally unloved. This is why I always felt close to my dad. I knew I could not totally give myself over to this man. He wasn't safe like my dad who I always felt would be there. My dad was my security. No matter how emotionally battered I was, I could go and spend time with my dad and feel all right about myself again—I had too much pride to tell them what was going on."

For a brief time, when her children were little, Mary again drew close to her mother who was ready with advice about the children from a mother's point of view. And her mother was usually willing to take the children and relieve Mary of their care. During this period, Mary still had some friends but didn't feel very close to them. The emotional drama of her life was being enacted solely with Andrew, her parents, and her children.

Mary, discussing her relational map of age thirty, described her son, Stanley, as very intelligent, someone she liked to talk to. She and her daughter, Lavinia, had "difficult times" because of Lavinia's tantrums. She found Lavinia hard to manage and couldn't understand what she wanted and what would set her off on one of her rages. "It took some time, but I brought her into line. She eventually became a really good girl." Then the third child, another daughter, was born—unplanned—and was a very "difficult baby." In a wonderful set of phrases, Mary describes her experience of motherhood. "I rocked Stanley because he liked it. I rocked Lavinia because she cried and I had to. I rocked Faith because I wanted to be sitting down."

With three small children, life was about getting tasks done and her friends were really just acquaintances who helped her when she needed help. Mary was still working at the church, but just part-time. She says little about her children at this stage of their lives except that she feared that Faith was "allergic to her mother. It was so hard to quiet her."

By age thirty-five, Mary was once again able to make room for some friendships in her life. She drew close to an old friend, Joyce, by helping her after her husband left her. She looked up to her neighbor Margaret—who was "a perfect *Farm Journal* housewife but not arrogant—she was an example." Her most special memory from this time was her father taking her to a conference at the college she had attended, where her sister was now a student. "He took me to a conference that my mother didn't want to go to and my mother kept the kids. It gave me a window on the world." Mary reviewed this experience in her mind many times and resolved to enlarge her world and find a way to have a place in it beyond being a wife and mother.

By the time she was forty, the two older children were off at college. She was especially proud of Stanley for being an outstanding student. "We'd read books together and talk about intellectual things. Even when he was at college, he'd tell me about what he was learning in his classes." She was pleased that Lavinia chose the same college where she had gone. "I thought she was turning out a lot like me," she said, somewhat dispassionately. Taking her there, Mary felt that she could become "part of things again."

Mary returned to full-time work. "I got tired of not having money I could have some say over. All my sisters-in-law were working, all the ladies I knew were doing something. I applied for a pretty responsible administrator job and, to my surprise, got it. Each morning I could be a well-organized efficient person who knew what she was doing—I felt capable."

When Mary was forty-eight, her mother died and she became extremely depressed, crying all the time. This was the only time in the interview that Mary wept. "I just didn't have with my mother the feelings that most people have with their mothers, and when she died I realized that I never would."

Mary had expected that when the older two children went off to school, things would be better at home, but things were no different. Andrew still came in from work and criticized everything. "I thought that with the two older children away and things quieter in the house, Andrew would be in a better mood. Then Lavinia announced she was going to get married but I didn't feel up to doing the wedding and couldn't think of any woman friend to call to help. I called my sister Wendy who came and did all the work of planning. She wanted to do it, so it turned out fine."

Around this time, Mary became "involved" with Keith, a man she met at work. "The first time he suggested anything, I said, we aren't those kind of people. He was a supervisor, he seemed to think I was wonderful, a perfect person. It was like salve on wounds for the years of criticisms. He's not cultured, but there's something about just being in the same room—I feel so supported emotionally. One day, it was like an electric shock just hit me. No one has ever found out. . . . There has never been any question about our being together. There was no way we would break up our families. We were surrounded by all these church people and Keith and his wife have been close to our family and our children." Surprisingly, though, things with Andrew went better after she began her relationship with Keith. "I could take the criticisms quietly because I knew there was someone who felt differently—knowing that someone feels that way about me has leveled me out a lot."

When her father died, though, she "felt like my rock was lost." Again she became depressed with periods of uncontrollable crying. There was also some relief: "I always worried that my dad would find out about Keith and would be disappointed with me." The only person in whom she has confided about her relationship with Keith is her sister Wendy. She is quite sure, though, that Andrew has never had other relationships with women. "He's too dependent on me socially," she says, somewhat triumphantly.

Looking back to age fifty, Mary laments that she still felt she did "not have any skills. I felt like I have no show and tell—what I do is always behind the scenes. I want a nice epitaph. After my father died, I began thinking about that. The church was packed after he died—everyone knew who he was." At this age, Mary had a special closeness with Faith, who had always been the one most distant from her. "Stanley is still struggling for independence from me. I've just adjusted to the fact that Stanley and I are not going to be as close as I would wish even though, growing up, he and I were closer." With Lavinia, she felt that they are always "stepping on each other's toes. Somehow whatever I say to her is wrong. I guess I've always been afraid that, although she is a really good girl, underneath there is something wild in her. She isn't married and doesn't tell me much about her life. Still, I know she loves me and that I am important to her. A daughter is a daughter."

Reflecting on her relationships from her current age, fifty-five, Mary describes the changes in her life. After her parents died and left her some money, Andrew was able to hire help on the farm. "I'm more convinced than ever of his love," Mary said. She made a new friend of a younger, more educated woman who has recently moved nearby. "There are so many things we think alike on. She is much younger than me, but I feel closer to her than women my own age—maybe because I don't have grandchildren to talk about. We have a real rapport. With the children being gone, I have to depend on somebody else for companionship. The ranks ahead of me have gone, too. I feel a sense of network. Maybe I now have more freedom to ask for contact with people. There's a farmer's group of husbands and wives who meet regularly every month. I feel part of a network with them. We have all gone ice skating together, which is something I used to do a lot when I was younger. There are ladies there I could call. I feel a warm supported feeling in this community—the minister and his wife—the church friends who have supported me and helped me. Even my hairdresser. When Faith got married quickly and unexpectedly, my friend Ruth told me she had done the same thing and explained that all Faith wanted was for me to be happy for her.

"Earlier in life, my security came from how many men I knew—my dad and uncles—and I never relied on close females—now I'm more headed the other way. Even Keith—as he retired, he's less free to move around, his health is not as good. So I'm coming to really appreciate my women friends."

For Mary, it feels like the story of her life has been a fight for freedom to be herself, a struggle that has continued in midlife. "That's been the most important thing. This is still my fight with my husband. He has certain ideas about how you behave—I like to break out of the mold once in a while."

Taking some distance from Mary's story, we can see that from an early age, she was attuned to people who "made a fuss" over her, did things for her, and made her feel special. Needing a sense of being special became the center of her need for others and she scanned her connections to others for how special they were willing to make her in their own lives. Mary primarily experienced this with her father and has, throughout her life, turned to men for this kind of gratifying response. Andrew's initial rejection of her when she was a teenager was therefore particularly wounding and, in some sense, the history of their long relationship has been one of enacting a dance of being wounded and then repaired. She married him to make up for the initial disappointment, to undo the damage, but then, throughout their marriage, she continues to feel verbally assaulted by him and then repaired by his nonverbal love. Keith is then another man in the chain who reassures her of her worth and she constructs him as a reincarnation of her father, the loving, approving, giving man.

Mary described her relationship with Andrew as being a "power struggle" and she seems to believe, at some level, that this is a struggle she has won. She says she never fully "gave herself" to Andrew because he never seemed to offer the security she felt with her father. Thus, by partially withholding herself, she triumphs over him. Mary continues to pursue her relationship with Keith, mindful that Andrew is too dependent on her to stray—or, perhaps, to notice.

Mary enacted in her own life the picture she formed of her mother—the long-suffering farm wife who was meant for better things. Like her mother, she felt stuck on the farm, taking in and caring for those in need. At the same time that Mary gave care, however, she resented having to do so—at least to women—and she recoiled from her daughters' need of her. She only enjoyed rocking Stanley; the girls she rocked out of necessity and duty.

Not being able to have taken in "special feelings" from her mother, Mary finds it hard to reach out emotionally to her own daughters. While she can experience Stanley as another man to impress and be special to, she feels somewhat mystified about what to do with her daughters, both of whom had seemed to her "difficult" to manage. Afraid of Lavinia's "wild" side, Mary treated her older daughter's impulses as she had always treated her own desires—suppressing them, trying to bring her into line to be the "good girl" that she always felt a need to be. Having struggled to figure out what to do with her own barely experienced "wild" urges to be other than what her social reality seemed to make available, Mary clamped down on these stirrings in her daughter. Today, she seems relatively uncurious about her daughter's life, except to wonder when she will marry and have children. We don't know what Mary means exactly when she says, "A daughter is a daughter," but it seems to point to expectations of continuing connection and responsiveness to one's mother, no matter what. Even when the relationship fails in important ways, the daughter can never really get away. The emotional tie of deprivation, as in Mary's case, who is moved to tears only when mourning what she would never be able to feel with her mother, is as strong a tie as any.

Mary says that she feels she has been closer to her daughters than her mother ever was to her, but she offers little evidence of this. Mary recalls the occasion of her wedding as the first time she felt any real closeness to her mother, as they girlishly planned all the details of the event. It is striking that Mary felt completely unable to join Lavinia in planning *her* wedding and in fact abdicated to her younger sister this role.

Mary seems to have been a dutiful mother, but her inner dramas were occupied with being special to men, men being the ones she elected to reflect her value and worth. Over the years of battle with Andrew, she had no doubt of her centrality and specialness to him. His criticisms of her emanated from his intense feelings for and need of her, and they served to initiate a drama of wounding and reparation that she and Andrew enacted again and again. Mary, of course, had as much a role in this drama as Andrew.

In finding new ways of being with women, Mary has constructed, at present, a comfortable life. She feels connected to others, embedded in her community and, all in all, she counts herself content.

LAVINIA

Nearly each time Lavinia, age thirty-four, mentioned her mother, from the first moments of my interview with her, she dissolved in tears. This meant that she cried through much of her narrative. Her first image of her mother was of herself taking care of her, especially when she cried. "My mother was lonely and in pain because of my father, and my job was to get her the aspirin, the glass of water and the Kleenex." Lavinia began her relational life story describing her brother, three years younger than she, for whom, from as far back as she can remember, she was the caretaker. "As my brother got older, he went out on the farm with my dad—I stayed in to help my mother—doing what she did." Lavinia described her father as a farmer who would get up early and come back late, and her mother was left alone with the children.

Lavinia interrupted her story at this point to explain to me that her father came from a "dysfunctional family." He was seventh of twelve children and "had a disciplinarian attitude about everyone in the world and he was sometimes abusive—physically, verbally, mentally. At thirty-four, I'm pretty much used to it. [Here she begins crying again.] Thinking about how it was at five, I was terrified of him. I was very upset that he acted the way he did—whether it was my mother or anybody. He was violent, directed towards everyone in the family—if it rained, it was upsetting for him. If it didn't rain, it was somebody's fault. Whether it was weather or the cows getting out or the combine breaking down, it was somebody else's problem. It wasn't just elements of nature, it was somebody's fault. We could never do anything to please him. He would go after anyone who crossed him and if mother tried to intercede, she would become one of the victims.

"My earliest memory was of him yelling and later it was explained to me that it was because I was getting ready to step on a hot furnace brace in the house. But I was two and I didn't know that and all I could remember was him yelling and scaring the daylights out of me."

How was he violent? I asked. "He hit, spanked." Yet, despite the violence, he was the one who would care for Lavinia when she was sick. "He would get up with me at night and get me aspirin. He was better at taking care of sick children than my mother, I think because of his experience of having so many siblings. He was caring and tender, despite the anger and the violence."

After her sister was born when Lavinia was six, she never sat on his lap again. "He'd still take care of me when I was sick, but there was no closeness. My sister was his favorite. She had bright red hair, like a lot of the people in his family. I learned recently that he never liked my given name—he always seemed to have a bad taste in his mouth when he said it—I thought it was because he didn't like me. It was my mother's choice and he never liked it."

Having no close neighbors, she and her brother played together during their childhood but had no other friends. Lavinia always perceived her mother as very lonely and turning to her for solace. "We started developing a friendship back then. I had to find ways to try to cheer her up a bit, like rubbing her back" (more tears).

Her memories of herself as a child are often set on her maternal grandparents' farm, fifteen miles away, where her mother often took the children. She had an aunt who was nine years older than she. "Sometimes I felt more like a late child of my mother's family. I was like a living doll to my aunt Wendy. I was there a lot during early childhood because my grandmother was better with little ones than my mother, so my mother would take us there during the days and we'd help with the canning, just being around my grandparents. My grandparents were very close to me. My grandmother would sit and read to us, hold us, talk to us about basic human elements, like love and kindness. She was more philosophical and religious than my mother, and very loving. A lot of a sense of community was instilled early on from the way my grandparents lived their lives and took care of others outside the family. My mother took care of us, but it was 'a different kind of caring'"—and here again, Lavinia cries.

"I remember those long conversations with my grandmother, but never with my mother. My mother was busy trying to take care of the house and I got to help with that. Helping her—that was our relationship."

Her father's family, Lavinia explains, was "sour, judgmental, difficult, and mean in their views of people. They were vicious in what they said about people and I never felt close to them." His family was also enormous, with forty-five grandchildren in her generation. In her age range, there were few girls except one cousin who used to beat her up. By contrast, the cousins on her maternal side were fun, cheerful, and happy.

When Lavinia turned ten, more chores were added. Now her father expected her to help with the milking and the chickens and her mother delegated to her additional housework. She joined the 4H club at school but was disappointed not to make any friends there.

At this age, she felt she was getting closer to her mother because she was learning to do a lot more to help her mother out. "I had to do a lot of watching 'the kids'—Even though my brother is only three years younger, they are saying 'the kids.' I'm 'mother's little helper, mother's assistant.' Anything my mother isn't available to do, I'm expected to do—laundry, ironing, I even started doing some of the cooking. That's starting around this age.

"I'm still seeing her in a lot of pain because of the violence. He's around, so if the cows get out, we're out there trying to get the cows back in and if it's raining, we're right there. If he's still out in the field at suppertime, we take supper out to him and it's very supportive. I see the supportive thing between my parents.

"I'm still afraid of him, even terrified sometimes, and he's still very caring, loving, and gentle when it comes to taking care of me and very, very loving with my sister and harsher with me. He expects me to meet his expectations faster and higher in taking care of him. If my mother's not there, then it's my job. And if I'm not doing it right, I'm punished. He is harsh with me. If I'm not doing it right, he yells—I'm not quick enough to respond to him. That was one of his biggest problems—if we didn't respond immediately." Here, Lavinia communicates some of the tension she experienced as she grew up—the need to be ready to do her father's bidding or be at risk.

Lavinia shared a room with her sister Faith, whom she felt got special treatment from their parents and "got between" her and her parents. "She could haul off and hit me but I wasn't allowed to touch her without her screaming bloody murder and I'd get punished. We were always fighting."

She and Stanley were still playmates, when they got to play. Lavinia feels that the more her parents expected her to be the assistant caretaker, the more division there was between the siblings. A real light in Lavinia's life before and through her teenage years was her aunt Wendy. She cries again thinking of how much she felt that Wendy loved them. "Wendy was really more like a half-sister. When she was coming over, it was going to be fun—we'd sing while we were doing the dishes."

Sometimes she felt that, with Wendy around, her mother would relax and be friendlier with her children, "but it was more cerebral than comforting." Lavinia watched her mother carefully and was attentive to her moods. She still felt like she had to nurture her mother, that her mother expected it since "she wasn't getting a lot of nurturing anywhere else— not from her mother or her husband." She recognized her mother's closeness to her own father (Lavinia's grandfather) and was glad that her mother took some comfort from him.

The carefree times of Lavinia's childhood were with her maternal grandparents whom she felt were constantly close, supportive, and loving. "We would go there and it was fun time, carefree, not much disciplining. They left us on our own. Their house was not very structured, and we had freedom from the rigid regimen of living with my father where he'd come home at a certain time and we would eat or we'd take him dinner in the field." The warmth of her maternal grandparents' home contrasted with the increasing gloom of her paternal grandparents' world. Her father's father seemed to get more cranky as he aged and Lavinia learned to keep an even greater distance from him.

Lavinia "hated" school. "I didn't fit in. I was weird, different, heavy. I was called Chubby Checker. The kids at school all lived in town, and I was on the farm. I went to church in one community and to school in another, so I had two sets of peers, but I wasn't close to either group. I had one friend, but it wasn't close. I was very centered on my family." However, participation in 4H offered her an outlet where she could feel appreciated. Her skills of sewing and cooking were noticed and rewarded.

When Lavinia was fifteen, her aunt Wendy moved back to their town, offering her a close confidante and supporter when she most needed one. "We were very close. She really understood all my adolescent dilemmas. There wasn't much she could do about it, but she was there, believed in me, was never critical and was just for me. Really, she was my anchor. I would go to her apartment after school, and stay there until she gets off work. But she's becoming more adult, dealing with her own stuff. And she's traveling, not there in person as much. After one year, she started graduate school and was back and forth a lot. When she wasn't there, I still talked to her a lot in letters, on the phone. We're establishing a long distance, but very much there relationship—advice, talking things out— she is the only person I'm able to do that with."

At this age, Lavinia remembers paying more attention to her maternal grandmother's ideas about theology, philosophy, and psychology and they had long involved conversations about the meaning of life. With her mother, she still found herself taking care of her a lot and sharing the responsibilities of the household. "I was kind of a rebellious adolescent, angry that the other kids aren't carrying as much responsibility in the house." They were more likely to be helping their father with farm chores. Lavinia had started also to get more involved with people her own age, largely through church and religion.

Through her church, Lavinia met Dick. "He was supportive, but there was also some weird stuff going on. He was my father's age, an ex-minister, but he was kind of strange in how he dealt with me at age fifteen. He was doing some paternalistic stuff like don't do this and don't do that, but he was also getting kind of friendly. I wouldn't say I was sexually abused, but looking back on it, I wasn't quite sure what to do about it. He was touching me, holding me, hugging me, and I hadn't gotten much of that from my father, and it was almost nice but meanwhile he was telling me I shouldn't let men do this to me. The only person I could talk to about it was Wendy. I didn't know what was going on, didn't know how to feel about it. I remember thinking, 'This is weird. The guy is married, his kids are my age. What's he trying to do?' And yet, he was the first nonfamily person that was really being supportive and caring and loving—in a real sense."

Something that troubled Lavinia a lot at this age was that her father's youngest brother, Archie, just seven years older than she, the only one of his siblings she was close to, had married a woman whom she really didn't like. She had long had a kind of a crush on Archie and felt he liked her in a special way, so Lavinia felt very jealous—both of losing some of Archie's attention and having to be around a couple that had the kind of investment in one another that she longed for. "I remember how angry I was when he got married and how much I hated *her*."

In her own nuclear family, she still felt treated like one of the grown-ups in contrast to Stanley and Faith who were "the kids." When her mother was ill or away visiting relatives, all the caretaking fell to her. "I'm still 'mother's little helper'—I am still the care-giving assistant to Mom and that was my relationship with everybody in the family." Her father was becoming more and more demanding and restrictive of her. "He's expecting me to be assistant Mom—except for actual marital behaviors. I'm following my mother's footsteps as far as following his demands and orders in housekeeping and all that goes with that and I'm also doing chores down on the farm. I don't like being with him—he's mean, angry, punishing, suspicious of anything. What he knew about teenagers he got from TV—if we moved too slow, he was convinced we were on drugs. That was his nature, to be suspicious and blaming."

Lavinia felt a need to stay close to her mother out of pity. "She had no friends and her relationship to my father was lacking. So I was really all she had."

Lavinia chose to attend her mother and aunt's alma mater, a church-related college four hours away from home. At age twenty she still felt her family to be the most important people in her life, particularly Wendy, who remained her confidante and advisor. She made some close friends at college, men as well as women, who were "nurturing, fun, accepting, not the kind of friends who would hate you for three weeks if you didn't eat supper with them." Spending her time with a group of friends, she didn't date but was involved in a lot of student activities. She struggled for a sense of independence from her parents by drinking occasionally. "There were times when my mother made a comment to me about if I was going to go out partying or something. I don't remember what the occasion was, but I finally said, 'You know, this is the way I feel about it and if I do go out and drink, I do drink on occasion, I act responsibly about it as you've always taught me to act responsibly about it.' They started realizing that I was independent and this kind of caused them some problems because I had always been so responsible and so goody-two-shoes for so long and never doing anything that could cause them grief, I think it was a surprise to them that I was declaring some independence. I think they were concerned that they were going to have to protect my brother and sister from this wild woman."

After college, Lavinia returned to her small Michigan town. At this time, her grandmother's brother became ill and Lavinia became his caretaker, not living with him, but checking in on him and spending time with him. "He was lonely—and we just got to be good friends. He sort of took me on as his granddaughter since he had no children of his own. I felt needed, looking out for him. He cared a lot about me."

Shortly after her return, Lavinia met Zack and they slowly drifted into marriage. "Neither of us had been able to meet anyone and his sister, who was married to my uncle, insisted we meet. There wasn't a lot of connection. He wasn't interested in religion, or in understanding that part of me. My grandfather once asked him if he believed in God, and Zack said no. I was sure that lightning would strike the house, but my grandfather just said, 'Oh, Okay.' I guess we loved each other because we didn't know what else to do. Two weeks before the wedding he said, If this doesn't work out, we'll get a divorce, so I walked down the aisle crying realizing that this was probably one of the biggest mistakes I'd ever made. And yet, looking back, it was a good experience. I learned a lot about construction and electronics, since we built a house together by ourselves, and getting used to someone different from me and I learned what not to do again with somebody else. We're still friends. If there's a technical problem, he'll come and help. He's a good person and a good man. I remember saying to my mother, 'What if Zack and I separate?' And she said, 'Well, I've managed to live with your father for so many years—you should have no problem with Zack.' And I said, 'Okay, thank you very much. This I have to handle on my own.'"

Her father still felt very far away from her, didn't understand her at all. "After two and a half years, I'm not pregnant, I'm not having babies, and I don't have a career. He had no idea what to make of me."

Lavinia's distance from her parents increased when she left Zack after being with him for three years. "He was too different from me. The only thing we had in common was the house we were building and it began to feel to me like I was building a tomb for myself. I wasn't ready to settle down in that house and live there for the rest of my life, so I left."

At twenty-five, Lavinia made her way to Chicago and began studying to be a chef. She found a close woman friend there, but when her maternal grandfather died, she worried that her mother had collapsed, and she dropped out of her studies so she could go home. Once this crisis passed, Lavinia returned to Chicago and was able to get a job cooking and started working her way up the ladder. She formed many close friendships with other women, who helped her through a personal crisis when she became pregnant and went through an abortion. The man she had been involved with "just disappeared. I guess I've always been kind of afraid of men.

They never treated me very well. And this one took the cake. I got pregnant and he just vanished."

It wasn't until Lavinia began having relationships with several men during her late twenties that she came to understand that Zack had been impotent. "I was so sheltered, I didn't know those kinds of problems. No one told me. I learned all kinds of things between twenty-six and thirty."

These years were a time of struggle career-wise and personally for Lavinia. She started psychotherapy but also recognized how much she needed her women friends to support her. She couldn't bring her troubles to her mother, since she thought of her mother as overburdened with her own problems as was, increasingly, her sister Faith.

At present, at age thirty-four, Lavinia is in a stable relationship with Dave, although he lives in Grand Rapids and they are together only on weekends. "We've been dating for a year and a half. He's supportive, he got me into ACOA [Adult Children of Alcoholics] attitudes about not falling into traps of dysfunctional family members. He's there, but he's very independent and I think we're still working on problems like how independent can we get, or how can we keep our independence and still merge this relationship. We're partners in being silly which I've never been able to be—just silly and joyous and just inner child fun stuff and sometimes we're like two kids playing. He's also the oldest child of a dysfunctional family and it's funny how we just click. Something happens and we look at each other and we just know what each other is thinking and it's more than I've ever experienced with anybody before."

Lavinia is now a supervising chef at a major restaurant and, although she works long hours, still has time for her close women friends. "I need friendships that are strong and supportive. We are all there for each other as cheerleaders. Not just work roles, but life roles." There are friends she looks up to and admires for their positive sense about living, but mainly for their support of her. At her current age, hers is a very peopled map.

With her mother, she feels she has gotten closer but is still trying to take care of her. "I'm working more at encouraging her to develop other friendships besides us, besides just the kids. And I'm trying not to run home every time she seems distressed. But I worry about her a lot" (more tears). Because of her involvement in ACOA through David, Lavinia has begun trying to look at her father as a person who is himself from a dysfunctional family and therefore not wholly responsible for how he had always acted in the family. She tries hard not to be angry with him anymore.

She feels distant from Stanley and Faith, who now live in different parts of the country, and is drawn to closeness with Faith only when Faith has problems and needs Lavinia's help. For the future, she hopes she and David can work out some kind of life together but expects that she will never have children. "I can't imagine being a mother, and I don't think I want to."

What was most striking to me in Lavinia was her emotional distance from other people. While she has relationships, they seem somewhat thin, superficial, based primarily on "support" which seems, to Lavinia, to mean that people are not critical of her and try to be accepting. She has developed insight into her own growth through ACOA concepts, which have helped her to think of her family as "dysfunctional." This, at least, has released her somewhat from her sense that she has to be her mother's caretaker and respond to family emergencies by sacrificing her own needs and interests. Her greatest pain, though, continues to be her despair at not being able to rescue her mother from what she perceives to be her loneliness and suffering.

CONTRASTING ILLUSIONS

Juxtaposing these narratives, we can see the disjunctures that are the hallmark of illusions. Mary and Lavinia paint strikingly different portraits of the same people, as they have experienced them in very different ways. Most telling is Lavinia's construction of her mother that is, as we can see but she cannot, a complicated mixture of her mother's qualities and her own imagination of her mother's situation. As a child, Lavinia somehow "read" her mother's pain in her marriage, but could not see the many layers of that relationship, especially not her mother's pleasure in it. Further, Lavinia has no knowledge, as an adult, of the way in which much of her mother's emotional life is lived with Kevin, her secret lover. To Lavinia, her mother's life is "just the children." Thus, Lavinia exaggerates her own importance to her lonely, oppressed mother and struggles within it and against it. This is the illusion that imprisons her.

Lavinia, for example, feels that she needs to "encourage" her mother to find other interests, but from Mary's point of view, this is precisely what she has been longing to do throughout her life and is succeeding in doing at midlife. Mary does not present herself (to me) as having the empty life that Lavinia believes she has.

Mary's sense that she and Lavinia "step on each other's toes" is not echoed by Lavinia, who continues to understand her relationship to her mother as one of taking care of her mother and getting little or no care in return. Lavinia, oblivious to her mother's subjectivity, does not experience conflict with her, only her own sense of deprivation and a sensitivity to what she perceives as her mother's calls for comfort.

Both women's lives have been marked by Andrew's mercurial nature. Where Mary saw him as critical and harsh, Lavinia saw him as violent and terrifying. Both also saw his loving and caring side, Lavinia in his caring for her when she was sick, Mary in his small gestures and sexual desire for her. Mary found ways to struggle against him and win the right to her own life while preserving her relationship with him. Lavinia emotionally (and physically) escaped from him, but paid the price of giving in to his demands for her to be a good girl serving his needs and being left with a mountain of rage.

Lavinia describes her father as physically as well as verbally abusive, but Mary does not say he was physically abusive. In fact, she does not use the word *abusive* at all. For Mary, he was critical and demanding, and she found a delicate balance between responding to his efforts to control her and subverting them. We cannot determine if Mary is denying to herself how abusive he was or if Lavinia is constructing her father out of her fears. Lavinia seems to have understood that her mother could not protect her from his demands; Mary never considers the impact he may have had on their children. She focuses only on her own thralldom to him and her inability to fully please him.

Mary, throughout her life, because of her own history, always took men more seriously than women. Although she had and still has close friendships with other women, it is clear that, in terms of her children, she most longs for a close connection with her son, the child who had most captured her interest as she was raising her family. It was Stanley she enjoyed playing with and talking to. The girls seemed always to want something of her she couldn't give and there were many ways in which she just didn't notice who they were or what they wanted, focused as she was on the needs and wishes of the men in her life—father, husband, son—and later, lover.

Lavinia, by contrast, grew up—and remains—largely frightened of men. It is not at all unlikely that, through the unconscious processes by which we create one another, Lavinia was chosen to "carry" Mary's fear of men. Mary has no awareness of her fears of Andrew—she paints him as someone to fight against for her selfhood. She is angry with him, but not frightened. She is the tough one, the fighter who suffers defeat but returns to the battle, while Lavinia expresses all the fear. When Lavinia, just before she married Zack, tried to express her fears to her mother, she was summarily turned away. As Lavinia remembers it, her mother could be of no help to her as she contemplated the difficulties of marriage, instead telling her, in effect, that it would be Lavinia's lot, as it had been her own, to manage it. Perhaps she could not empathize with Lavinia's anxiety because it was too close to her own repressed fears.

Mary and Lavinia similarly paint very different portraits of Mary's mother. The history of nurturing among the three generations of women in this family twists and turns. We, of course, do not have the story from Mary's mother, but it is interesting that Mary brings her children, especially her eldest child, Lavinia, to her own mother for care. Indeed,

Lavinia finds her grandmother much more nurturing and loving than her own mother. Mary ends her story with tears about what she never received from her own mother, but although she doesn't realize it, she arranged for her daughter to be the beneficiary to receive what she never did. Mary's mother is, from Mary's point of view, distant and unresponsive, but from Lavinia's vantage point, she is the loving, involved one.

To hear Mary tell it, her own mother was incapable of offering the love she needed. But is this because she was preoccupied with her disabled child, as Mary sometimes thinks? On the other hand, Mary was quite besotted with her father and seemed to prefer him as a parent. There could, then, have been some underlying competition between Mary and her mother that led Mary to experience her mother as rejecting her, or perhaps actually led her mother to reject her. Mary's mother was, however, able to give to Lavinia a "closeness" that her own daughter had longed for from her. Lavinia, of course, is experiencing her grandmother in contrast to her father's family. In this comparison, her maternal grandmother is clearly the more nurturing one and it is perhaps Lavinia's readiness to respond to her as a loving other that draws this capacity from her. Mary's mother is an important figure in both of these lives, but the lenses of illusions, constructed from bits of experience as well as fantasy, cause her to appear very differently.

Mary seemed to have had little interest in mothering her children or in the quality of her mothering. Having children was part of what was expected, as she says. She was overburdened by the tasks of running a farming household. She felt stifled by a culture that seemed to offer her little opportunity for self-development and a husband who demanded that she fulfill a script written by his family. She wanted mainly to avoid his criticism, but she does not portray herself as Lavinia saw her—as crying for years. She does not even say that she had been sad or depressed, only frustrated and overworked. It is important to note here that Lavinia describes her mother as always in tears, but it is Lavinia who cries throughout the interview. We might wonder if one unconscious conversation between Mary and Lavinia is over who would cry the tears in this family—tears of deprivation, tears of anger and hurt feelings, tears about there being not enough love to go around.

Lavinia could only feel a connection to her mother, a connection she desperately needed as a child, by feeling that her mother needed her. By being "mother's little helper," she felt herself in a unique place in her mother's world. Her mother's need of her gave her a reason for being. Beyond this being her assigned role, there are also deeper psychological and emotional strands to this connection. In effect, Lavinia ended up bonding with her mother by giving to her mother what she wanted her mother to give to her. This is a common form of unconscious relating, in which one person treats the other as they wish to be treated by them. By attending carefully to her mother's moods and trying to supply what she thought she needed, Lavinia was giving to her mother the "support" she desperately longed to be given herself. Although paradoxical and indirect, it can nevertheless be a fulfilling and compelling way of unconsciously "creating" the other: "You exist for me to take care of you as I wish you would take care of me and my taking care of you creates the emotional connection between us. Then I need not wish anything from you."

From Mary's side, Lavinia seemed to be good girl and didn't cause her trouble, but she was never intriguing to her the way Stanley was. Mary just assumed that Lavinia would be like her, that she would follow along in the sequence of women in her family, and Mary squelched Lavinia's assertiveness in the same way she did her own. When Mary had Wendy take over the role of listening to Lavinia and teaching her, Mary felt freed of the burden—one less chore to attend to. Andrew assigned Lavinia to be Mary's helper and he settled the disputes if she rebelled. From Lavinia, Mary could remain emotionally disengaged.

There are haunting parallels between these women's lives that may point, nonetheless, to Mary's unconscious scripting of the niche for Lavinia to occupy. The most important woman in Mary's early life had been her aunt, the one who died when Mary was eleven. Her aunt had been the source of solace and comfort and this continued in Mary's fantasy life long after she died. Therefore, it made emotional sense to Mary that Lavinia would turn to *her* aunt, Mary's sister Wendy, for the same kind of support and love. Her inner templates of relationship were patterned for this configuration of support—the distracted mother, the involved, loving aunt. It is as though the script called for an emotional distance between mother and daughter to be filled by mother's younger sister. While this felt expectable to Mary, Lavinia, who never even knew of her mother's relationship to her aunt, experienced it as a rejection by her mother, but a rejection born of frailty rather than hate.

Both accepted the premise that you have to marry when you have the opportunity or miss out. This is how Mary framed her decision to marry Andrew and also how Lavinia spoke about her marriage to Zack. Lavinia, however, once she found herself "entombed" in her mother's script, abruptly left the set—and it is not clear how she found the courage to do this.

Neither woman expresses any disappointment at the end of Lavinia's marriage and Mary, while maintaining the idea that Lavinia is just like her, may also have wished for Lavinia to do something very different. Here Lavinia's name is worth pausing to consider. Mary, who has what was the most common of names in her generation, gave her first child, over Andrew's objection, a very unusual name. (Lavinia is the name of a character in the children's book *A Little Princess*.) This is perhaps a sign that Mary may have harbored the romantic hope that, in some way, Lavinia *would* find a different path. It is thus possible that there was a second, hidden script.

Interviewing these two women in the same week, I was struck by how they are each in their own way in search of self-development, in fostering friendships with other women and enlarging the scope of their worlds. But they don't share these pursuits with one another. They remain unaware of the similarity of their struggles to feel valued in the world. Common to both women is the contrast between being in the world of the family and being in the larger world. For Lavinia, it was not until she moved to Chicago that she developed relationships that "counted" in her life, independent of family members. College allowed her to rehearse having friendships, but she didn't develop what she could feel to be meaningful friends until after she left home a second time. For Mary as well, her life was lived largely in the family, despite a few efforts at friendship in college and after. Not until midlife did Mary create friendships that felt lasting and emotionally enriching.

Across both generations, this is a family in which feelings are not discussed. Emotions are carried in the atmosphere of relationships. Both Mary and Lavinia draw the same portrait of the two grandparental families—Mary's family as interested in ideas, playful, and warm while Andrew's family is somber, cranky, critical, and puritanical. When Lavinia left Zack, she did so because she found herself in an emotionally empty space although she could say little about what their relationship was like. It wasn't until she met David, who took her to ACOA meetings, that she found a vocabulary to talk about what she had been experiencing in her relationships. She learned to think of herself as having been "a parentified child" and that her caretaking of her mother was a form of "codependence." These phrases were meaningful to her because they helped her articulate the inchoate atmospheric oppression and the chaotic feelings that swirled within her and to think about who she had been in her relationships. It has also helped her name and speak her anger at her father—once she could classify him as dysfunctional and abusive. Having these phrases in a supportive context of people who seem to share her experience has helped her build a sense of autonomy where she is less buffeted by the roles that others have assigned her. Her views of her parents, however, stay crystallized in their unchallenged illusionary form.

We must also wonder about the illusions Mary maintains about herself. She does not recognize that in her own way, she may have behaved as imperiously toward Lavinia as Andrew did toward her, expecting care as her due, making unrelenting demands—subtly rather than overtly. However, Mary wards off such a possibility, depositing all the "demandingness" and "expectations" in the family in her husband. She speaks as though she had no needs or expectations from her children, although Lavinia experienced her as incessantly demanding.

There is, of course, no "truth" about these two women. There is only their construction of one another—both as they have created one another and imagined each other. They are bound in love as mother and daughter—but *who* they see and think they love represents only a few sides of a complex figure. Lavinia has "created" her mother's weakness and helplessness in two senses. By seeing only her mother's loneliness and enslavement, she constructs her mother in her own mind as a beleaguered, depressed, and lost woman in need of her care. In addition, caring for her "creates" her mother's helplessness by offering her a daughter to lean on and treat as an extension of herself whom she doesn't have to notice as a truly separate person. This, in turn, creates an emotional bond between them, a bond very difficult to break or alter. Therefore, when her mother is grieving the loss of her father, Lavinia feels impelled to return home, giving up her own nascent effort at independence. Lavinia could not allow herself to see the passionate bond between her parents and could only imagine her mother as a victim trapped by her father's demands. Further, Lavinia is at a loss to imagine that her mother has an emotional life beyond her need for Lavinia's care.

Mary needed to squelch any sign of independent or passionate action from Lavinia, for this reminded her of her own unrealized needs for self-assertion in the world. Mary's fears of Lavinia's potential "wildness" came from fears of her own inner states. Early on she experienced Lavinia's cries as a burden and demand and could not tell what she needed, much as she could not know what she herself needed. Thus, she "created" Lavinia in her own image, as a good girl who asked for nothing for herself.

Each of these women would dismiss the other's view of her as unfounded in "reality"—and as unfair. For Lavinia to see her mother's striving to make a mark in the larger world and to be independent of the family would mean she risked losing the emotional rope of caretaking that yokes her to her mother. In effect, to feel that her mother no longer needs her would mean to become motherless in the world. For Mary to acknowledge the deprivation Lavinia has felt from her would mean to be back with her own critical, depriving mother, but now with no loving father to salve the pain. It would also mean to acknowledge her own capacity for emotional coldness and unrelenting demandingness. Thus, each has a blind spot in regard to the other, a blind spot that they cannot psychologically afford to illuminate. Each must retain her illusion of the other to sustain her sense of self. But in doing so, they can never reach or really know one another.

6

Secure Knots: Tom and Kathy

When I see couples, even long-married ones, I often feel that the first order of business is to introduce them to each other. Who each thinks the other is can be very different from who the other feels him or herself to be. Tom and Kathy, happily married for a while, had each looked to the other to "be there" for them while they pursued their other interests in life. They each wanted the security of a "rock," someone they could take for granted to always love and cherish them. And both unconsciously agreed to enact the part in order to feel safe themselves.

Tom, a tall, somewhat owlish, twenty-eight-year-old doctor, initially consulted me after his wife, Kathy, left him. He spoke slowly and deliberately and rarely looked me in the eye. He was depressed and confused about what had gone wrong in his marriage. Because he was so unclear on what he had done "wrong," Kathy agreed to meet with me to tell me her story. From both, I obtained a full relational history, which allows us to see how these very different characters intersected and constructed one another.

TOM

Tom grew up in what he describes as a close family. His parents were wealthy and involved in the high society of Baltimore, but he remembers his mother being very attentive to his needs and those of his brother, Bill, who was just ten months older than he. He had a sister, Nicole, six years older, who doted on her baby brothers, and a childless aunt and uncle,

101

sister and brother to his parents, who pampered the boys. "I always felt very loved by everyone, except Bill—we fought all the time." Tom describes his father as "the disciplinarian. You just didn't cross him. He never said much, was at work or playing golf most of the time, but when he got home, we all kept out of his way. But we really admired him. He was an important person, and was always getting honors and awards."

On his relational maps, Tom draws his parents as interlinked with one another, at some distance from him and his siblings. "They were a unit. They had their own world, lots of socializing and were absolutely devoted to one another. My father only ever really wanted to be with my mother and when he was around, she thought about nothing other than pleasing him. They are the happiest couple I've ever known."

Tom then told me the story of his parents. "My mother was a debutante, came from a really important family in Baltimore, and my father was a hard-working lawyer, from a good family, but not as prominent as hers. My mother had everything except for one problem—she was kind of homely. She just isn't pretty. So she was getting to be almost thirty, which in that time was really old to marry, and no one had asked her. Then her brother married my father's sister and at the wedding, she started spending a lot of time with my father—and they fell in love. I think she was just so grateful that he could really love her and married her that she has been willing to do everything for him ever since. And he—he just loves her."

Tom describes himself and Bill as each half of one whole and therefore different in every way. Where Bill was outgoing, athletic, and musical, Tom was shy and studious. Bill loved to perform and be noticed and Tom thinks he was always his mother's favorite. But Nicole, their sister, preferred Tom, so he always had an ally and a refuge. The two of them together would play pranks on Bill and then cover for each other when Bill tried to protest to their parents.

Tom's description of his early years sounds like an idyll. "We had everything, did everything. My mother was always there, except when she was off with my father. She was a baking bread and gourmet meals mother. Sometimes they'd go on trips, but we had a live-in babysitter, so things didn't change too much. Still, I didn't like it when she went away."

When Tom was ten, he had a group of friends who liked to collect bugs and do science experiments together. He and Bill were in different social circles and barely spoke to one another. Again, Tom describes a life without conflict and disappointment during this time.

Beginning with middle school, both boys went off to boarding school, which Tom describes as a wonderful experience. He again had a group of friends whom he liked being with and doing things with. He was focused on doing well so he could go to Harvard, which is just what he did. Although the family was a warm place to return to on school holidays, and although he appreciated the "care" packages of goodies his mother sent each month, he didn't think much about the family; life was lived in the academic demands of the school and the camaraderie of his friends.

Bill is drawn at the periphery of Tom's map. "We just didn't have much to do with each other. Sometimes we wouldn't even go back and forth to school together. We were in different circles. People couldn't believe that we were brothers. When we were home, Bill still got more attention from my parents. He was a good talker and could tell stories and amuse them or play the piano for their friends to sing along. I was more to myself, but I could always talk to Nicole. My parents were always scrupulous about giving us money equally, and I knew they loved me. If they came up to school to watch him play football, they were always careful to try to include me and ask me a lot of questions, but I knew they were there because of him. Bill was more flashy, always was, but it really didn't matter to me. I was smarter than him. I had nicer friends. I knew I was going to succeed."

The only family crisis of his history occurred when Tom was fifteen and back from school for the summer. To everyone's shock, they discovered that Nicole was pregnant. As the family was Catholic, abortion was out of the question. In addition, the father was an older man, non-Catholic, a man outside their social circle, and there was a strong sense that Nicole had brought disgrace on the family. For the first time, Tom saw anger, recrimination, and tears in his family. "My mother was beside herself. My father wanted to disown her—at least, I think that's what he was threatening. But in the end, they made them get married quickly and move somewhere else until after the baby was born. But what I most remember was my father calling me and Bill into his study, shutting the door, sitting behind his desk, staring at us sharply, and saying, 'If either of you *ever* get a girl pregnant, I want you to know that you will no longer be welcome in this house.'"

When Tom was sixteen, he fell in love for the first time, with Samantha, whom he thought of as "pretty, smart, funny—and she adored me." Samantha was from a nearby boarding school and also from Baltimore— so they could see each other both at school and at home. His life revolved around her, every free minute. "Of course, my parents didn't really approve of her. She wasn't from quite the right family, but they didn't exactly interfere." They had wonderful times together until Samantha abruptly broke the relationship off after two years. "We had gone to different colleges, but still saw each other on weekends and during holidays. I have no idea why she broke up with me. She just dumped me," he says with some bitterness.

Feeling burned, Tom dated a few girls for the next year but felt mistrustful. "Whenever I went out with a girl, I'd try to figure out if she was

a dumper or not." When he was twenty, he met Kathy, a brand new fresh-
man at Harvard, and she seemed to have all the qualities he wanted in a
girlfriend—and he trusted her. "I just knew she was the One. I met her
and I just knew. But when we first started dating, there was a time that I
got worried that she was a dumper, too, so *I* dumped *her*. Then I was sorry
I did that and got back together with her—and I didn't want her going out
with anyone else." After dating for three months, he bought her an engagement ring. He wasn't ready to get married just then, but he wanted
them to be a couple. Whenever he wasn't in class, they would be together,
studying together, going for pizza. They liked each other's friends, so
they often had fun together with others.

   Although they enjoyed "making out," Tom, who was still a virgin,
didn't want to have intercourse with Kathy until they got married. He remembered his father's injunction, was aware that all birth control measures have some failure rate, and just didn't want to take the risk. "I could
wait," he said. "I think this was okay with her. We could still have sex, just
not intercourse. But that wasn't the main thing in the relationship, at least
not for me." Sometimes he thought Kathy was too demanding of his time.
"It's like she couldn't delay gratification. If she wanted to do something,
she wanted to do it right then, and a lot of the time this interfered with my
studying. I had to study a lot. First, I was applying to medical school, then
I had to make it through medical school. She didn't have to study as much
as I did. So sometimes this was a source of conflict. I liked her to be at the
library studying with me."

   On his age twenty and age twenty-five maps, which are nearly identical, Kathy is drawn intersecting him and larger than any other circle except his own. By this placement, Tom meant to indicate that she figured
most in his life.

   Tom was aware that his mother didn't approve of his choice of Kathy,
particularly as the relationship got more serious. His mother had her eye
on a number of daughters of friends in their social circle and her hope was
that Tom would return to Baltimore and marry within their community.
Kathy wasn't from the upper class. She was at Harvard on a scholarship
and was interested in having a career herself. She didn't at all fit the image that Tom's mother had for a good wife. "But I told her I would marry
who I wanted to marry and that she'd better start liking Kathy since that's
who I was going to marry."

   Tom got close to Kathy's parents. "They were completely different from
my parents—just very simple, but very loving. I began to see all the pre-
tense in my family, all that caring about what other people think and
keeping up appearances. In Kathy's family, we could eat at the kitchen
table with paper napkins and play Monopoly together at night. Her
mother was a teacher and we could talk about ideas, not just gossip about

people like my mother always liked to do. I guess at this age, I was starting to get critical of my own parents and started to see some of the artifi-
ciality of their society life. I knew there is no way I wanted to go back to
Baltimore and fit into their world. For my twenty-first birthday, my parents gave me a membership at their country club, which is the last thing
in the world I wanted. I returned it to them and told them I had no interest in this. Bill kept the one he got when he turned twenty-one."

Throughout college, Tom remained close with his high school friends,
who had also gone to the Boston/Cambridge area for college. His closest
friend from boarding school was in his college at Harvard, and he and his
buddies played golf together, watched reruns of fifties television shows,
and often had parties with their girlfriends together on weekends. He describes these friends individually in warm and humorous terms; they
were all "buddies," companions, people who helped each other with
rides, muscles, money, whatever was needed.

When it came time for medical school, Tom chose to study at Harvard,
which worked out well since Kathy still had two more years there. Once
Kathy graduated, they got married. "I wanted us to be like my parents
were in terms of their devotion to each other. I treated her a lot like my father did my mother. I always got her nice gifts for her birthday and for
Christmas, took her special places for dinner, called her whenever I could
from the hospital or the library. I loved her. I thought she loved me. I
thought we had a really good marriage."

"It was a complete shock to me when [two years after they married] she
told me she was leaving me for another man. I just can't understand it. I
told her I'd do anything so she'd stay, but she wouldn't even try. Maybe I
was too rigid. I think now that I've turned out like my father, but I never
wanted to be that way. But I'm really angry that she wouldn't even give
me a chance to change."

Of course, Tom felt betrayed by the knowledge of Kathy's affair, but he
blamed Paul for spiriting her away. He could not imagine that there was
something within Kathy that sought fulfillment elsewhere. He still
thought that Kathy was the wife he always wanted and could not think
that she had changed—or perhaps never was who he thought she was.

In Tom, we see a relatively clear example of someone who set out to
find a pre-scripted character to be central to his life—a loving woman
who would play the same role for him as (he thought) his mother had for
his father. He called this role "the One." Only vaguely concerned with
whether or not this was who Kathy wanted to "be," Tom was confident
that he could enlist her to the part he had in mind for her.

Tom's life had been filled with people who provided him with what he
experienced as a safe, uncomplicated kind of love. Although Tom uses the

word *love* frequently, he never asks too deeply just what it means. It seems for Tom to refer to people who are constant, reliable, warm, and available to him, people he can trust to be "there" for him and have good times with. Used romantically, it seems to mean devotion. Throughout his life, he was able to attract and maintain loyal friends. He had no problematic relationships with anyone except his brother, and he dealt with this conflictual relationship by distancing himself as much as possible.

When Tom recruited Kathy to play out the role of the loving, constant wife, he wished to duplicate the uncomplicated kind of loving that he was accustomed to. He wanted Kathy "there" for him but was not too interested in exploring who she was as a person. Tom wanted to take his relationships for granted while he pursued his dream of being a doctor.

Taking his sense of self and identity from his studies and his career goals, Tom doesn't look to others to validate him or reflect him. He thrives on companionship as a break from his studies, or at least, wants to have companions available when he wants to relax. His relational dreams are, from an outsider's point of view, perhaps somewhat stereotyped. He wants what he thinks he saw between his parents, echoed in the popular culture of the fifties—the Cleaver family, from *Leave It to Beaver,* one of his favorite TV shows. He had no interest in exploring the complexities of relationships; he regarded his own family of origin as being exactly what it appeared to be, no emotional undercurrents, no hidden agendas, although as a late adolescent he became critical of their values. If his mother preferred his brother, well, then he would be content with the special attention of his sister, without, it seems, resentment. If his brother, the musical performer and athletic superstar, was overflowing with popularity, then Tom didn't mind. He simply pursued his academic success, enjoyed his friends, and had his own version of a nice life.

Tom's equanimity is admirable in many ways, yet it appears that he gained this emotional peace by recruiting people to play emotionally undemanding roles. He had no insight into why his first girlfriend abruptly left him and understood this by categorizing her as a "dumper." But when Kathy left him, he succumbed to a kind of terrified confusion—something was going very wrong in his relationships and he had no idea how to understand it. Now he feels like a blind person suddenly given sight who is bewildered about how to meaningfully decode the light that suddenly floods him.

Tom is an attractive, appealing man (in my view). It seems that if he had done better casting for the role of wife, his life might have worked out as the smooth sailing he envisioned. In some ways, this is what Tom also believes.

From Tom's description, we see Kathy only as the perfidious wife. From Tom, we have little sense of her as a person. Therefore, I needed to meet Kathy to learn about Tom.

KATHY

Kathy was a tall, curly-haired, serious young woman with luminous blue eyes who, when I first saw her, was very anxious and conflicted about where her life was going. Full of guilt about leaving Tom, she was trying to make sense of how she had found herself in what was to her the humiliating position of getting a divorce.

Thinking back to age five, Kathy remembers herself as a fearful child whose feelings were easily hurt, and she thinks of herself as almost clinging to her mother. "I don't know what I was afraid of, but I know I cried all the time, and I always wanted my mother. Even when I was ten, I still wouldn't go up the stairs to the bathroom unless she came with me. I was afraid of the dark, among a lot of other things. If I wanted a glass of water at night, I was afraid to go get it and I would call her."

Kathy describes her mother as "the most wonderful of mothers. She never criticized me, was always loving, was always there for me, no matter what it was. I hear other girls complain about their mothers, and I just feel so lucky." Growing up in a fairly strict Catholic family in a small town outside of Baltimore, Kathy's life was structured by a father she experienced as authoritarian and demanding. "You didn't cross him. Whatever he said was the law, and I was always afraid of him. He never hit us, but I was terrified when he would get angry. But he really loved me. He was a down-on-the-floor playing kind of father and I loved to sit on his lap and have him read to me." Kathy had a younger brother, but they were never close. "I think I never really wanted him to be born. I always resented him. I needed a lot of attention and didn't like his getting any of it. And I always felt like my father treated him specially because he was a boy." At age five, Kathy remembers her relational life as secure and warm. She had a loving grandmother and doting aunts and uncles. As the first child in the extended family, she felt very special.

On her relational map of age ten, Kathy begins a saga of longing for friends. The love that flowed in her family was difficult to obtain outside. From age ten on, Kathy's maps contain many dotted circles, representing people she was intensely engaged with in fantasy but had little actual contact with. "There were not many kids in the neighborhood, my mother didn't really have friends with kids my age and I never felt liked by the other kids in school. I was always feeling left out. I guess I was pretty shy and my feelings were always easily hurt. My mother used to say that if someone looked at me cross-eyed, I'd cry. So at age ten, I remember being at home a lot, kind of bored, because I wanted to be playing with people my age. I remember always nagging my mother and father to play board games with me. I hated playing with my brother. He was too little to really understand the games, but usually if they played, he had to play, too.

I guess it was around this age that I started to imagine a best friend and would make up stories in my mind about the things we would do together."

Between ages ten and fifteen, Kathy's life was dominated by her struggle to be liked by the other kids. Gifted intellectually, Kathy was always at the top of the class, "and it was not cool for a girl to be smart in those days. Feminism hadn't gotten to Small Town, USA yet." Her parents took pleasure in her academic success, but Kathy worried that getting branded a "brain" made her even less popular with the kids at school. "I did my schoolwork, but all I really thought about was who was nice to me that day and who didn't want to sit with me at lunch. At night, I would always replay the day in my imagination with a wonderful friendship with someone who I liked a lot, someone who liked me, wanted to be with me, noticed me." In seventh grade, Kathy made a best friend of Cindy, who was also somewhat on the margins of the social world. "At least it felt like we were isolated together, and Cindy became the most important person in my life. I would spend all evening on the phone with her, until my father yelled at me to get off the phone." Kathy's relationships with her parents continued to feel secure. Her mother understood her struggles and was someone she could always talk to about her disappointments in her social world. "I remember having long, long talks with her at night as I helped her with dinner and then cleaning up. I'd tell her everything that happened during the day and she was just really involved in everything in my life. She was a teacher, but she always had time for me." With her father, Kathy learned to pretend compliance while hiding a lot of her activities. "He tried to control me, but never really succeeded. I never let him know about a lot of things. And my mother would cover for me."

When the girls in her class started to date, Kathy again felt left out. "No one wanted to date the smart girl. I thought I was unattractive, out of it. I cried a lot at night." Kathy comforted herself with elaborate fantasies and crushes, making in her imagination a world where she was popular and in demand. "Naturally, I was the one without a date to the prom. There were a few guys I had gone out with, guys from another school, but they were never the ones I really liked, or if I liked one, he didn't like me enough to ask me out again. I was sure I was doing something wrong with people, but I could never figure out what it was." Cindy remained a close friend at age fifteen, and she also made a new friend of Megan, one of the more popular girls. Megan always had a lot of boyfriends and Kathy tried to learn from her how to be attractive to guys. But the fact that Megan liked her and was willing to be her friend was a boost to Kathy's view of herself.

Going off to Harvard on a scholarship changed Kathy's life. "I was determined to have a different life. It was like getting a second chance, starting over in a place where no one knew who I had been. And I would be with other smart people, so I didn't have to feel like so much of a freak anymore." As college began, Kathy found herself in the midst of a social whirl she had always dreamed about. One day she had four dates—for lunch, study date in the afternoon, dinner date, and then another study date. "But the funny thing is that this just confused me. I think I didn't know how to handle it. It was kind of overwhelming. I was the kind of person who was used to going over in great detail in my mind every interaction I had with anyone. And this was just going too fast for me to sort it out. I didn't know who liked me or why or if I liked them. It was all just kind of happening."

Then, in the third week of college, Kathy met Tom. "He was a junior with a car and very, very nice. I was young; I had just turned eighteen. He knew his way around and helped me adjust to being away from home. He took care of me. He seemed to really like me and to want to do things for me. He had money, took me nice places and seemed to want to spend all his free time with me. For several weeks, I pretty much just saw him. Somehow he made me feel safe. I didn't feel nervous about him. Then, after a couple of weeks, he abruptly broke up with me. Just said he didn't want to see me anymore. I was devastated—I felt I had started to rely on him and then I couldn't trust him. I felt like no one would ever want me. A week later, he called me and told me that he had been thinking about it, that I was the girl he really wanted, that he was sorry for breaking up with me and that if I went back with him, he promised that if our relationship ever ended, it would be because I decided to break up with *him*. And I knew he was the kind of person who could keep this promise. I wasn't sure what I wanted, but I started seeing him again, along with other people. And somehow it was his reliability—he was like a rock. If he said he would pick me up at 6:30, he was there exactly at 6:30, not 6:29, not 6:31, but 6:30. One day he was walking me to my mailbox and I said I was sad because I hardly ever got any mail. From that day on, every single day for six months, even in the middle of a big snowstorm, there was a card in my mailbox from Tom. A couple months after the breakup, he took me to dinner and offered me an engagement ring. He said we wouldn't get married for a couple of years, but he wanted us to be engaged. That was an important moment in my life. I didn't really want to be engaged, I wasn't sure I wanted to be engaged to Tom—after all, he was my first real boyfriend. But I didn't know how to say no gracefully and I thought that if I said no, he would leave me. So I figured I would take the ring and could always give it back later."

But the "later" never came and Kathy married Tom when she graduated from college. "Tom steadied me. He was like a warm blanket, kind of like my mother had been—always there for me if I needed anything. I was still having lots of fantasies about other guys, but I figured that that's all that would ever come to—fantasies. At one point, I even had a crush on Tom's brother, Bill. I knew that none of these guys would ever want me. And Tom was, in his own way, quite desirable. He was good-looking, rich, smart and he adored me. But we never had any real intellectual or emotional connection—I never felt I could tell him my deeper thoughts and feelings. I had girlfriends for that, though. My parents thought he was terrific, my mother said he was 'a good catch.' In many ways he was the man of her dreams. There just never came the right time to break up with him.

"Once I almost did. Eight months after we got engaged, there was this other guy who I was having a lot of fantasies about. We worked together on a project and he wasn't attached to anyone. I really wanted to go out with him. Over some weeks, I was preparing how to tell Tom that I wanted us to take a little break, just to make sure we were right for each other, but I was really afraid of hurting his feelings and losing him. Then a good friend of mine broke up with her boyfriend and a couple of weeks later decided she had made a mistake. At this point, though, her boyfriend didn't want to go back with her and she was in agony, feeling that she had ruined her life. Going through this with her, I thought, I don't want this to be me. And what if I go out with that other guy who was really not as desirable as Tom, and then I lose Tom. . . . And there wasn't anything wrong in my relationship with Tom. It's just that there wasn't any passion—although he did a lot of romantic things. I don't know. I couldn't figure out what was wrong, but I knew that life was a whole lot better in those years with Tom than it had ever been before I met him. My parents were thrilled with him. He easily became a part of my family and I was delighted that he was able to see their good points even though his family was high society and mine most certainly was not. He grew up in a mansion. By contast, my house was a hovel, but I really believed that in some ways he liked it better.

"The year before we got married, I fell wildly in love with one of my teachers, Harold, a section leader. I thought about him all the time and lived for the moments I could go to his office hours. Tom had no idea about this, but my best friend did. She thought something was weird about this and used to ask me what I thought I was doing, but I just felt like one was my real life and one was my imaginary life. A month before the wedding, my teacher, Harold, asked me to dinner to discuss some work we had in common. When he brought me home, he kissed me, something I had dreamed about incessantly. The next day, we met to talk about what had been going on between us. I just couldn't get my mind around calling off the wedding. The invitations had been sent out, my life seemed planned for me. Harold wasn't handsome and rich—he was kind of a confused guy. I went to the mental health clinic, but the therapist there told me I probably had some pre-wedding jitters. Mainly, though, I was so afraid of being alone again, which is what I was afraid would happen if I broke off with Tom. With Tom, I always had someone. So I went ahead and married him."

Kathy describes her marriage to Tom as good. "I had a sort of difficult relationship with Tom's mother. I knew she didn't want Tom to marry me and in some weird way, this increased my determination to do it. Kind of 'I'll show you.' But she is a well-brought-up lady and once we were married, or it was clear we were going to be, she was never anything but polite to me. I think she tried at times to get close to me but her way of doing this was to tell me what to wear and how to change my hair, but when I made it clear that I wasn't going to let her remodel me, she backed away from me all together. I really liked Nicole and got along well with her and her children. So Tom and I fit in well in each other's families."

At ages twenty and twenty-five, Kathy's maps brim with relationships. Highly involved in college life, she made many friends. Her roommate, Annie, had become a new best friend, whom she could talk to about "anything and everything." Kathy discovered that she could be likeable and interesting to people and she felt she was "glowing" during these years, with both academic success and social fulfillment. "I no longer had to imagine friends. I had many of them, great friends. I couldn't have imagined anything better. There was always someone to call and do something with if Tom was busy studying or at the hospital and there were always long, deep conversations about life and feelings."

Kathy and Tom were both busy with their studies, but they had friends as couples to have good times with on weekends. "Life was good during this time. We didn't really see much of each other, but we were happy together. There was someone else I was fantasizing about all the time, but it wasn't as intense as it had been with Harold, who I never saw again."

Between ages twenty-one and twenty-five, in graduate school studying psychology, Kathy found, within her graduate school class, a number of people who became close friends. Kathy described these new friendships as "pretty intense." The group was interested in psychoanalysis. Feelings and fantasies were legitimate parts of experience to talk about endlessly and Kathy found a vocabulary for things that she had felt for a long time but couldn't find words to express. "We'd spend hours analyzing ourselves and each other and it was both scary and exciting. We'd also talk a lot about our patients and about other people in the class, and somehow I felt all my ideas about people beginning to change. It's like all my old categories about the right way to be and to live began to crumble."

I asked Kathy for an example of this. "Like my friend Rina had an enormous effect on me. She was like a free love kind of person, always with erotic adventures that we'd laugh about together. This is kind of embarrassing to tell, since you will see how sheltered I was. We were both working for one of the professors in the department and he took her along to a big conference to help out. When they got back, she told me about how he tried to sleep with her and I just didn't believe her. 'But he's married and a professor,' I said. 'He probably wouldn't really have done it.' Rina just laughed at me and told me I was an incredibly naïve good Catholic girl. Now I realize how right she was." Kathy had long given up practicing Catholicism, but she was learning to what extent she was still a small-town girl with romantic, provincial ideas about people.

During graduate school, Kathy also began to form friendships with her professors and this was very gratifying to her. They were models to look up to as well as people to have intellectual conversation with "but kind of as equals. They were interested in what I had to say and this gave me a lot of confidence."

She found a mentor in one of her professors, Daniel. He took a special interest in her and secured a special fellowship for her. She was thrilled that such an important, distinguished scholar could think her promising and take her under his wing. They spent long hours in conversation walking along the Charles River. "Daniel could make me laugh longer and harder than anyone I had ever known in my life. We had exactly the same sense of humor. And I learned more from him than any amount of classes or reading. What I became was completely because of him." Eventually, she fell in love with him and thought he was the most perfect and interesting person she had ever known But he was nearly thirty years older than she and, although she enjoyed flirting with him, she couldn't imagine a life with him. "And I was close to his wife, too. I just couldn't even fantasize a life with him. He was older than my father. I think I really wanted him to be my father. I don't know what I wanted from him. I remember one night, Daniel, his wife and I were sitting in their TV room watching the Patriots on Monday night football and I felt like I was in heaven. It was the most amazing feeling of contentment. When I thought about this later, I realized I didn't want to be there as his wife—I wanted to be his child. My own father was not intellectual; I don't ever remember seeing him read a book. I was now in a new world, a world very far from my parents. And I wanted Daniel to be my protector, which he was, but I think that being in love with him was . . . I don't know what it was."

The new world, represented by her studies in psychology, changed Kathy "profoundly." All her ways of thinking about people seemed challenged and upended. "My mother, Tom's mother—all they talked about was the right way and the wrong way to act. No one ever looked deeply into others' motives. They didn't really believe that the unconscious influenced what we did. They didn't understand psychology and still thought that therapy was for sick people.

"Among my friends and teachers, people talked about relationships all the time. Actually, they talked about sex all the time. I wasn't sure what the big deal was about sex. I had been raised Catholic and very sheltered. Tom and I didn't have sex until after we got married. I guess I started to wonder if I was missing something. And I started to wonder if having these fantasies all the time was normal." In graduate school, where she was the youngest woman in the class, Kathy enjoyed her classmates and teachers flirting with her. "It was like I had become a sort of femme fatale or something. I looked great at that age—twenty-three—and I began to realize that some of the excitement I was feeling, and all the fantasies I was having—I was in love with Daniel at that time—probably had something to do with sex. Tom was in his last year of medical school, working hard and exhausted most of the time, so we hardly ever had sex and when we did, it wasn't exciting at all. One night, I remember, he even fell asleep as we started to make love. So then there was this guy, Paul, a fellow student, who I also had a crush on and he was really flirting with me all the time and I was starting to think about him a lot and then one day he asked if I'd go to bed with him. I was so straitlaced at that point, but also curious. My first response was, How dare you? What do you think I am? But then I was really curious and wanted to be a kind of woman of the world like my friend Rina, so I told myself I'd do it just once, just to see what all the fuss about sex was about. And that's how I discovered sex, I guess. What happened with Paul had nothing to do with whatever it was that Tom and I were doing. Somehow all the passion and fantasies came together with my body and it was a whole new world. We had this incredibly intense affair for a year. Sometimes we went to lunch, but mainly we spent hours and hours in bed, making love, talking, making love over and over again. It was incredible. Tom never suspected anything. As long as I did the things he expected me to do—cook his meals, iron his lab coat, be nice to his friends on weekends—he was completely out of touch with me emotionally. If I ever tried to talk to him even a tiny bit about what I was feeling, or even learning about people in my psychology classes, he just had no patience for it. He'd just say, 'What's the bottom line here?' Then Paul was about to get his degree and move away. I couldn't be without him. But I couldn't be without Tom either—he was my rock, my security.

"They are so different. Tom is absolutely giving, but Paul is absolutely exciting. Here's an example. One week, I was out to dinner with Tom and he got a cherry in his drink. 'I love maraschino cherries,' he said, and handed it to me. Later that same week, I was out to lunch with Paul and he also got a cherry in his drink. 'I love maraschino cherries,' he said, and ate it. This story tells it all. Even though I loved Paul passionately, how could I give up Tom—he was always so good to me."

In the midst of agonizing about her decision, a crucial event occurred. While wrestling one day, playfully, with Tom, Kathy's eye was injured and she was taken to the emergency room in Boston. Scared and in pain, Kathy had to decide whether to allow the doctor to perform a surgery on her eye. She didn't trust this doctor and didn't want him to treat her—but she was in pain. She turned to Tom, who was, after all, a doctor, for advice. But he just backed away and told her she had to decide. Later, Kathy looked back at this as a crucial moment. "I realized then that I was on my own. He couldn't really take care of me. When it came down to it, he was more worried about seeming to overrule a fellow doctor than he was about my eye or my fear." Tom thereby lost his role as her protector. And that made it possible for Kathy to decide to leave him.

"I felt horribly guilty about leaving him. He is a good person. He just isn't right for me and never was. I hate it that I hurt him. It's not his fault. I grew up and he didn't. He needs someone who is content with a simple, quiet, ordered life. Lots of women would give their soul for something like that. But I need someone who I can talk to about my feelings, who is interested in the inner world and who is deeply sexual and passionate. My relationship with Paul isn't perfect, but it's satisfying in so many ways. I don't have fantasies about other men any more. I realize now that there are trade-offs between security and excitement. And I don't feel as secure with Paul as I did with Tom. He left his wife for me, so I guess that's a pretty big commitment. It's possible that this won't work out, but I'm not quite as afraid of being alone. I think I could manage on my own, at least for a little while. But I think we can make it together."

At age twenty-six, her current age, Kathy has four close friends on her map, women she feels she can confide in and who share her struggles and her joy. "They support me. I couldn't have made the break with Tom without them. Annie even let me live with her after I left Tom and was waiting for Paul to find us an apartment. I talk to Cindy [her oldest friend] nearly every day." Kathy's mother did her best to be understanding and supportive of her choice. "She wants me to be happy, but she can't really understand what's wrong with my marriage to Tom. To her, if a man doesn't drink or beat you and makes a nice living, he's a perfect husband." Kathy's father was furious at her and didn't even try to understand her reasons, so they haven't spoken beyond hello and good-bye ever since Kathy moved in with Paul, whom he refuses to meet or mention.

THE LINKED SCENARIOS

As we juxtapose the stories of Kathy and Tom, we find two people who each thought they had found in one another what they most needed—a sense of security. They drew together initially in order to overcome their individual fears of rejection and to reconstitute an early feeling of unconditional love that could be taken for granted, a love each had experienced in childhood. Tom, although he cannot verbalize it, must have unconsciously sensed in Kathy a deep insecurity about herself as a woman which he learned he could quell with his stolidity and certainty. By being a rock for her, he felt that he had tethered her to him, and he had been in search of someone to be a constant, devoted presence for him. After his first disastrous love affair, Tom simply wanted someone who wouldn't leave him, someone he could count on for the long term. Uninterested in the subtleties of relationship, Tom had wanted a partner to be there for him when he was ready to turn his attention away from his career strivings, someone to organize and manage his life outside of work. Unconsciously, Tom repeated his parents' scenario—his father rescuing his mother from her homeliness and earning her eternal gratitude and devotion. In his case, he rescued Kathy from her social anxiety and fears that no man would ever find her desirable. For Tom, marrying Kathy settled things, rang down the curtain on his drama of searching for a partner. He married her believing they would live happily ever after. If Tom sensed the restlessness and internal angst in Kathy, he chose to ignore it, in hopes perhaps that it would either disappear or be unimportant. He simply assumed that Kathy's commitment to him would be as durable as had been his parents' commitment to one another and to him.

There was a two-dimensional quality to Tom's description of relationships throughout his interview. People were simply what they appeared to be—either trustworthy and constant or else disagreeable people to be avoided. Like many men, he forged close emotional connections with others around shared experiences like watching sports on TV or going on outings—experiences to share and then talk about, usually with humor. For him, intimacy was uncomplicated—"either she loved me or she didn't"—there were no gray areas, no places for ambivalence or emotional complexity. And because this was his model of the characters on his stage, he wanted Kathy to be similarly clearly etched. He spoke frequently about how a wife "should" be, as though his wishes were self-evident requirements that any worthwhile person would embody. ("She *should* understand when I am tired or have to work. . . . She *should* be dressed nicely when I get home from work.") There was no room in his script for her changing if that meant altering her relationship to him. He wanted her to be as predictable and constant as he felt himself to be, and he wanted her to enact his script of devotion as he had seen it in his parents. Thus, Tom had cast Kathy in the role of "my perfect wife" and responded only to those aspects of her. He assumed that he had cast well and that she would fulfill her part.

For Kathy, Tom appeared at a time when he served to vanquish her fears of being left out and alone. "Once I was with Tom, I never had to

worry about having a date for the football games or to see a new movie."
Although aware that "something was missing," Kathy just continued her
childhood pattern of creating fantasies to fill in the gaps. Fearful that she
would never find anyone who would love her, Kathy tried to content herself with a half-full glass. She had, with Tom, recreated her relationship
with her mother, the warm, "always there" person who doted on her. And
Tom was also, like her father, the demanding man she could seem to
please while hiding important aspects of herself from him.

In college, Kathy's view of herself as unlikable and unattractive began
to change (in part because of her emotional reliance on Tom) and she began to feel more confident of her ability to draw people toward her. In
graduate school, Kathy began to acquire a deeper understanding of herself and others and, hesitantly, started to wonder about the choices she
had made. While she had always appreciated Tom not pressuring her
about premarital sex, she now began to view him as sexually inhibited. Influenced by the sex-focused atmosphere of her graduate studies, Kathy
gave herself permission to explore her own sexuality—and this was never
part of the script that she had created for Tom. Kathy had, in effect, cast
Tom in a role in a play that she no longer wished to take part in. "I just
didn't want to be the long-suffering self-denying doctor's wife anymore—despite my mother's advice that with Tom I was 'set for life.' I
wanted some spice, some adventure, some passion, someone who would
at least try to understand me—and those are things Tom just wasn't
about." Therefore, the day in the hospital when she lost the illusion of
Tom as the ultimate protector, the role her parents had seemed to occupy
in her early childhood, shifted the ground on which the relationship was
built and it became impossible for Kathy to continue in it. Kathy had
recreated herself and was in search of other characters with whom to
script a new drama. The scenario with Tom had finished its run without
either of them ever really knowing the other.

But Kathy is learning that, unlike in fantasy, where we can make people do whatever we want, real people have inner lives and dramas of their
own which they are eager to live out, but these are opaque to us. Conse-
quently, real people behave in ways outside of our control. She is cur-
rently struggling with Paul's unpredictability. "I know he loves me, " she
says, "but it's important to him to have some freedom as well. Sometimes
he comes home late and doesn't want to say where he's been. He wants
me not to ask and I find this really hard. With Tom, I always knew exactly
where he was and what he was doing. I'm not sure I can be with someone
who needs to make me this anxious. Sometimes I think that Paul likes it
when I get anxious about him. He likes it when I am jealous." Kathy and
Paul are in the process of negotiating who they will be for one another.
Since they are openly together and she can no longer cast him as the "se-

cret, wonderful lover," Kathy is trying to find a new role for Paul that fits one of her emotional scripts. Already she is imagining him as a womanizer, fearful of his intense sexuality, although (or maybe because) this is what drew her to him. Increasingly, Kathy senses that Paul has a script that includes the anxious, jealous woman waiting for him at home and she is not at all sure that this is a role she wants.

Tom, meanwhile, was left with the dilemma of having to reconstruct his model of the world and refashion it to one that includes ambivalence and emotional complexity, something he doesn't really want to do. His dramatic stage had been colored just in black and white—things either are or they aren't, and life unfolds in epic fashion, leading only to success or failure. It was difficult, as a therapist, to persuade him that there are other dramatic forms, multilayered forms with shadings and uncertainties. What Tom wanted most was to find someone new to fit the role rather than to reconstruct it—or himself.

It was hard for Tom to believe that Kathy really hadn't been the woman he had thought she was; he could not see his role in constructing her this way. (Tom's explanation was to blame Paul for spiriting her away, thus keeping Kathy good but weak in character.) And Kathy simply believed that Tom is a dogged but dull man—that she both found him and left him as he essentially *was*.

As I got to know Tom better, though, I began to discover the ways in which Kathy kept him as she needed him to be at the time. Tom reported that Kathy, as she was leaving him, complained of his sexual inhibition. But, Tom protested, when he tried to be sexually playful and passionate, she rebuffed him (which, of course, reinforced his own shame in regard to sex). "I even offered to go to sex therapy with her," Tom told me. But in this couple, it was sexual inhibition that partly glued them together. Tom's fear of sex, inculcated by his father's stern warning, intertwined with Kathy's naïveté to lead them to a sexual relationship that was sexual in behavior but not in feeling. When neither of them was at all discontent with this, neither had to ask to whom the inhibition belonged. They were able to not notice the mechanical nature of their sex life and their lack of interest in it. Or, if either had thought about it, they might have attributed the disinterest to the other ("He's always too tired." "She never seems very willing.") It was only the press of the sexualized atmosphere in graduate school that led Kathy to explore "just once" what she sensed she might be missing. And then she began to locate all the inhibition in Tom. He was juiceless; she was erotically afire. At this point, needing him to "hold" her inhibitions, the psychological economy made it impossible for her to invite him to join her quest.

When he tried to be spontaneous in other ways, Tom felt, she looked at him as if he had gone crazy and sternly seemed to admonish him to act

his age. Thus, Tom felt, Kathy insisted on his being just the way she complained that he was. This is a very typical process in couples. Whatever
one most dislikes in the other is usually not only what attracted him or
her in the first place but what he or she unconsciously manages to keep
fixed in the script. Therefore, unless we can witness the projective and il-
lusional processes involved in such a relationship, we are left with only a
superficial understanding of it—an understanding that regards each person as simply "being" who their partner regards them as being.

Sometimes the depth of projections and mutual creation is so en-
trenched that no amount of insight will change it. This seemed to be the
case with Tom and Kathy. If they could no longer imagine the other as a
kind of steadfast bedrock of security on which to anchor a life, if they had
to confront the other as complex and struggling human beings, they could
no longer be needed characters in each other's inner lives. But both took
the opportunity to learn something about the ways in which they are
prone to create certain kinds of others and to be scripted by others in certain ways. In therapy, Tom struggled with looking at people as composi-
tions of opposing qualities rather than as the unidimensional, uncomplicated, committed beings that he wished them to be. Eventually, however,
he found another woman, Emma, whom he felt could be "the One" and
asked her to marry him after knowing her just a few weeks. Tom was still
unable to tolerate ambivalence in others and could only attach to someone he could believe was in some way "his." On the other hand, Emma
seemed to regard him as sexy and lively, which made it possible for him
to access these parts of himself in ways he could not do with Kathy. With
Emma, Tom was feeling very passionate and even wondered with me
once whether Kathy just didn't like sex.

I saw Kathy again twelve years later. I will relate more about her fate in
the next chapter, but the later contact also gave us both more insight into
her construction of Tom. In later years, Kathy was to learn about her
propensity to "become" whatever others wanted her to be in hopes that
they would reciprocally "be" her fantasy of them. If the other person was
attractive to her in some important way, she was eager to secure a part in
their script, no matter what it involved—just as she had done with Tom.
In order to guarantee the security Tom promised her (in words and
deeds), she had been willing to enact his "perfect wife"—not consciously,
of course, but she easily learned the part. But then, she was to discover
through more experience of life, Kathy would, after some time, have to as-
sertively protest that she was more than what others had made of her.
Rather than trying to counter projections in a new relationship by saying
"Hey, that's not who I am—but this is," Kathy had learned to personify
the wishes she sensed in the other, as if she were saying to other people,

especially men, "Okay, so this is what you want—this is what I will be. Whatever it takes so you will stay with me." Her relationship with Paul seemed to be posing new challenges in this regard and it was not clear at the time how she would resolve the difficulty of his not enacting the "security" she had left with Tom, the predictable man she had wanted and cast away.

7

Pygmalion and Galatea

Kathy and Paul's relationship foundered and ended after a year. Then twelve years later, now nearing middle age, they meet.[1] Each has a marriage and a family. They recall nostalgically the intense passion of their relationship, the sexual heights that neither has ever reached since. "I don't know how you made that happen," says Paul, "but I still like to think about how things were between us." "How *I* made it happen!" exclaims Kathy in astonishment. "It was you who made it happen. It was *you* who introduced *me* to sex." Paul just shakes his head. "That's not how it was at all. Maybe I was the match. You were the fire."

This conversation encapsulates the conundrum of our creation of one another. Paul and Kathy discover that they had each credited the other with being sexual catalysts, enlivening them to their own passion. In each of their relational life stories, the other is the "demon lover."

Who we are to the other is not identical with who we are to ourselves—and who others are to us is not who they are to themselves—or, for that matter, to other people. As we go through life, we fit people we encounter to unconscious scripts from our inner library even as we take up a part in theirs. There is no way to know what "really" is because the whole fabric of relationship is woven in mutual illusionary processes.

We project onto and into people aspects of ourselves and our earlier experiences and then have a hard time modifying what we have decided is true of them. In fact, Paul hadn't been out womanizing—he was only working late. Since Kathy had constructed Paul as sexually gluttonous, and since she knew that he was perfectly capable of lying about his sexual behavior (as he had lied to his wife about her), she became convinced

121

that he was out with other women. And Paul, for his part, had experienced his mother as intrusive, never allowing him any privacy. He didn't want to have to account to a woman for his whereabouts. These were the "realities." But, with our deeper understanding of these processes, we may also wonder if Paul hadn't been assigned to embody Kathy's sexual duplicity (about which she was extremely guilty) or if, on Paul's side, he hadn't unconsciously chosen Kathy to reenact his mother, provoking her suspicions so she would try to control him and he could resist her control.

ILLUSION AND CREATING THE OTHER: THE BUILDING BLOCKS OF RELATIONSHIP

The illusory processes of falling and being in love are the most dramatic examples, partly because the intensity of the feeling stands out vividly against the more measured emotions of other kinds of interpersonal experience. And romance always involves idealizing illusions. But the processes of constructing the other occur in precisely the same ways all along the continuum of love and hate, through all the subtle gradations of human experience. Indifference, the emotional opposite of love, marks the absence of any construction of the other. Indifference is the absence of meaning. As soon as we begin to ascribe meaning to a relationship, thereby making it emotionally real, we engage our "inner playwright" to provide the script, the costumes, and the makeup.[2]

Illusion is easiest to see in others, of course, when our perception is not clouded by our feelings. The processes through which such creations evolve are more difficult to bring into focus. As we have been able to see by juxtaposing these four paired relational autobiographies, the processes of mutual creation take place outside of awareness in subtle and highly nuanced forms. Among members of a family, people are born into existing potential scripts, and children are assigned roles to enact based on the unconscious needs of their parents, themselves products of scripts to which they had been assigned. Yet similar processes occur in all relationships—between friends, in the workplace, among neighbors, and so on.

An old maxim says that when we truly need a teacher, a teacher appears. The same is true for needing a lover, a friend, or a rival. When we encounter a new person, we are mutually casting, reading very subtle cues to see if the person can fit some (often unconscious) role we have available—and they are regarding us in the same way. This is often referred to, when consciously apparent, as "sizing up" the other, but it is an affective, rather than a cognitive process, an extension of the mutual attunement process that takes places in infancy. Neuropsychologists understand this as occurring between right brains (Schore, 2001). If we need to be a savior, we find and create someone who seems to need protection and rescue; if we wish to submit, we find (or create) the dictators in and among others. By inducing others to be what we believe they are, we stock the dramatis personae of our lives. Only if there is some match, some mutual recognition that gives meaning to the other, does a relationship begin to evolve. Relationships are created as they are discovered and discovered as they are created.

If we pay attention as we interact with others, we notice that there are many layers to the messages that people send our way. Every relationship implies a definition of self by other and other by self.[3] This complementarity can be central or peripheral and can have greater or less dynamic significance at different periods of one's life.

Interpersonal reality is a chaotic mélange of layers and layers of emotional and interactional signs. Any single interaction with another is loaded with potential meaning—even a simple "good morning." There is an old joke about two psychoanalysts who meet in the elevator and one says "good morning" to the other; the other gets off the elevator thinking, "Hmm, I wonder what he meant by that?" As with most humor, there is an important truth here. We all interpret, at some level, the "good mornings" of our lives. How was it said, with how much warmth, with what kind of feeling, with what invitation (or not) to pursue the interaction? Think of how many times you have heard a "good morning" and decided the person was cool, distant, or angry or the "good mornings" that seemed to you flirtatious, interested, and full of the promise of something exciting to come.

The feelings that others express toward us are multilayered and blurred and sometimes underground, even to the person him/herself. Only in very rare social contexts is it acceptable to say "What did you mean by saying 'good morning' in that way?" without sounding foolish or paranoid. Most likely, our acquaintance was unaware of expressing other than a pleasantry or, if he or she is aware of something more, unwilling to bring it to light at the moment. Our interpersonal reality, then, is usually structured in such a way that we must "guess" at the subjectivity of the other. And we reorder our own feelings and take action based on an accumulation of these conjectures which, gradually, over time, begin to solidify into a sense of "reality"—how that person *really* feels about me, or what that person is *really* like. Further, once we have created our image of the other, later experiences tend to affirm it in such a way that we more and more believe in the essential externality of our internal representation.

Illusions can be quite impervious to reality checks as the psyche works to maintain its equilibrium, which requires a continuing conviction in the simple existence of the treasure that has been "found." Billy Wilder's classic parody of gender roles and illusions, *Some Like It Hot*, ends with a hilarious comedic send-up of this impenetrability. In this film, a much-married wealthy older man, Osgood (Joe E. Brown), has become enamored of Daphne (Jack Lemmon posing as a woman) who, seeing an opportunity for money, leads him on. The film ends with Osgood, determined to marry Daphne, driving them off in a boat, while "Daphne," recognizing the impossibility of the situation, tries to disillusion him by pointing out that "she" is not what he thought she was.

Daphne: *Osgood, I'm gonna level with you. We can't get married at all.*

Osgood: *Why not?*

Daphne: *Well . . . In the first place, I'm not a natural blonde.*

Osgood (looking ahead and maintaining his self-satisfied smile throughout): *Doesn't matter.*

Daphne: (knowing that Osgood's mother broke up his last marriage because his wife smoked): *I smoke. I smoke all the time.*

Osgood: *I don't care.*

Daphne: *I have a terrible past. For three years I've been living with a saxophone player.*

Osgood: *I forgive you.*

Daphne: *I can never have children.*

Osgood: *We can adopt some.*

Daphne: *You don't understand, Osgood.* (Pulling off his wig and throwing it down) *. . . Ehhhh . . . I'm a man!*

Osgood (not looking at him, continuing to drive the boat, still smiling): *Well . . . nobody's perfect.*

(Credits) THE END[4]

"Doesn't matter, I don't care, I forgive you, we can work it out." All of these are strategies for maintaining illusions in the face of facts that don't fit. Ultimately, nobody's perfect, which is a way of saying that I will maintain my illusion despite anything. Yet, having just shown us the other couple in the story (played by Tony Curtis and Marilyn Monroe) happily snuggling in the back seat of the boat, Wilder seems to underscore that our illusions drive our lives and we cannot live without them.

As we interact with others, we read messages about who we are for them and we send messages about who we expect, want, and need them to be for us. The messages we read include aspects of their emotional and psychological state at many levels of their experience. The surface content of what they are telling us is only the most apparent. In addition are all the signs of how they orient themselves to us, who they feel we are for them at that moment. In any statement from another, we can read the dynamics of power and intimacy between us, their complex feeling states about us, about themselves, and about the matter at hand. In response, we do two things. First, we selectively attend to certain aspects of the communication, usually those that are in line with the "illusion" we have of that person, how we are expecting them or needing them to be. Second, in response to that person, we are reactive to certain levels of their message and not to others. In responding selectively, we unwittingly amplify these aspects of the person by pressing them into our pre-cast mold. Like a good director, we have to maintain control over the actors on our stage to make sure they play their parts well.

When illusions take root in the other, we can think in terms of creating the other, that is, projective identification. This takes a bit longer than it does to form an illusion and requires sustained interactions such that the needs of one person have an impact on the psyche of the other sufficient for the other to "become" and live out the induced script. Recruiting others onto one's stage involves bringing psychological pressure to bear on them by stirring up strong feelings in them, tapping into their longings, fears, and internal conflicts.

The processes of creating the other are organized implicitly and affectively. Although we read the stories of relational experience narratively, we more sense the meanings inherent in them than deduce them from the events. Similarly, co-created relational worlds are beyond conscious verbal experience and lie in the realm that Bollas (1987) calls the "unthought known." They are sustained by countless exchanges that both create and reflect the relational construction. Heirs to the kind of preverbal exchanges between infant and mother,[5] they are the atmosphere, the grounding of the relationship.

Creation of the other is an interactive process—the press of one person's unspoken, unconscious needs interweaving the availability of the other to live out the projected image—and the corresponding availability of the first person to be in the required role on the other's stage. Where there is a match, the other leaps readily onto the stage to enact the expected role (McDougall, 1985). Kathy, for example, sensed Tom's need for security, and she produced her capacity for loyalty and steadfast predictability in order to "be" the faithful, immutable other that Tom needed her to be. Tom's fears of aloneness sparked her own and they forged an unconscious pact to protect one another. Bringing only her promise of safety to the relationship, Kathy muted other aspects of herself that did not fit Tom's script. Only later, apart from Tom, could she experience herself as adventure seeking and novelty-hungry and indeed, eventually partnered with a shy, somewhat fearful man who relished living through her daring. With her new partner "holding" her anxieties, she was also, then, able to take more risks. Similarly, as we saw, children "become" parts of their parents, and siblings apportion the internal dilemmas. People in the workplace "become" the rebel or the sycophant, as needed, and friends "help" each other by expressing the other's disavowed parts.

It is not an easy task to distinguish our own subjectivity from what has been projected into us or imagined by the other about us. Since we actually "become" what others would have us be, the boundaries between what aspects of ourselves derive from authentic wishes and feelings and what we absorb from others can be quite murky. Thus, Joan's struggles with self-expression feel to her like they are inherently hers. She does not recognize their origin in her father's conflicts. And Donna and Roberta have each perennially been confused about whether her needs for care and rescue belong to herself or her twin sister.

Psychotherapists who work with couples or groups encounter these processes most vividly since couples often bond through locating parts of their internal world in the other and a group tends to assign difficult affective states to particular members. Here we can consider a commonplace vignette from a couple: Carolyn tells her husband Roy in a warm and wistful way (or that's how it sounds to the therapist), "I wish you spent more time at home." Roy reacts here to what he experiences as Carolyn's controllingness and begins to detail all the work obligations that make it absolutely necessary for him to spend exactly as much time as he needs to at the office. In this comment, Roy selectively attends to Carolyn's wish to have him do what she wants and does not hear her affection or wish for intimacy. Roy is, therefore, overreactive to Carolyn's "controllingness," which leaves her in doubt about whether indeed it is this part of herself that is in the forefront. Roy reacts in this way because of some earlier sensitivity he has garnered to being controlled or because he needs to perceive himself as pulling away from a woman who is trying to hold him back. In doing so, however, he may be amplifying her controllingness by giving her the message that he will not respond to her needs or show interest in trying to please her. The only recourse she may have then is, indeed, to try to exert more control, thus "becoming" his controlling other. But there is yet another possible explanation of this interaction: Uncomfortable with his own needs for intimacy, Roy may unconsciously assign Carolyn the role of "speaking" the need for closeness so he can both express and repudiate his own conflict-laden feelings—and the interaction may be more about intimacy than control. He may, in effect, be telling her to keep knocking on his door while simultaneously telling her to go away. The performance of this conversation, a repeated scene from their marriage, sustains their definition of their situation (Goffman, 1961) in which she demands and he withdraws.

Through these intricate unconscious conversations, we may create the very qualities in others that we imagine to be there. This can be put to good use when we "see" positive aspects of people and our noticing what is good in them calls forth these aspects. To some extent, Carl Rogers's contribution to psychotherapy, which advocated unconditional positive regard for the client, served to strengthen those good aspects of people that had gotten buried under what they experienced to be mountains of devaluation and criticism. "Believing in" someone can engender his or her strengths. To return to an earlier example, the Helen Hunt character in *As Good as It Gets* enables the Jack Nicholson character to "want to be a better man" by seeing the good in him. Sometimes we can use these processes to bring out the best in each other.[6]

When processes of illusion and creating the other are central to our emotional stability, we have a stake in keeping the other people as we experience them to be and find it difficult to represent them to ourselves as whole human beings with significant experience apart from us—that is, as independent subjects. In designating people with possessive honorifics— *my* mother, *my* brother, *my* wife—for example, we name them by their role relationship to us, thus, at least at some level, speaking the fantasy that they "are" identical to these roles, that they exist as aspects of our own experience of them. In her autobiographical novel, *The Shadow Man*, Mary Gordon (1996) tells of her quest to know the true history of her adored, adoring father who died when she was seven. What she finds is a person very different from the one she felt she knew. "The man I know is a man I gave birth to. His name is not David. . . . It is My Father" (p. 194). Here Mary Gordon reaches the awareness of having given birth to her "father"— that is, her illusion of him. When we take someone in possessively, as "my," we gain what seems to us to be an unshakable connection, but we also lose our capacity to regard him or her as a human being beyond our construction. Mary Gordon's quest was "Who was the David for whom being a father to me was a part of his life?" This is a question that most of us would find hard to bring to any of those people who are most important in our lives; the fear is to discover all the aspects of their existence that are *not* in relation to us. Days before my much-beloved mother died a few years ago, I was able to record her narration of her life story. I was somewhat unsettled to hear that I was not the main character—actually, a fairly minor one, although I know she loved me very much. It was perhaps a testament to the openness of our relationship that she could narrate it *to* me without coloring it *for* me. In addition, I had some glimmer of recognition that all the people who had mattered to her throughout her life were also a part of me as well. She had created me, as I had created her.

Keeping in mind (empathically) independent subjectivities taxes our capacity to embrace complexity. If it is difficult to do in relation to just one other person in an intimate relationship, the problems of doing so in regard to groupings of people are exponentially greater. The processes of creating the "Other" extend to wider social groups and are what make it possible to define the boundary of one's own group. The other becomes a repository for all that is devalued within the confines of the in-group. "They" are the ones who are immoral, lazy, aggressive, or evil. "We" are not. We regard these others as an undifferentiated entity and find it hard to understand their (multiple) motives from their point of view. Even as a group as large as a nation, we may subtly evoke "bad" actions on the part of the other, creating an enemy, so that we can reassure ourselves that we are "good." Simultaneously, we produce a focus for our (disowned) aggression. At the level of societal analysis, these complex processes account for vilification and combativeness between groups (e.g. Volkan, 1997 and 2004; Young-Breuhl, 1996; Rice, 1965, Gillette and McCollom, 1995).

VALENCE: THE READINESS TO BE CREATED AND DISCOVERED

People are not totally malleable and there are some limits to what one person can script another to be. Although everyone possesses all aspects of human potentiality, the astute director must cast the right sort of performer. The wisdom of the unconscious "finds" others whose own unconscious needs resonate to the projective, illusionary needs we have, people who consent to be cast into the roles we have in mind.[7] If there is not the expected and needed (nonverbal affective) response, we try someone else.

Over time, certain people find that they are likely to be scripted by others in particular ways, that is, to have a valence for certain kinds of roles. In a group, some people are the ones who are customarily chosen to do the emotional soothing or to confront others. In close relationships, similarly, some people are habitually the ones to give in, to do the planning, to express the anger, or to crack the jokes. We saw how Mark, for example, was, throughout his life, chosen as a leader, chosen to be the responsible one whose judgment could be relied upon to be unclouded by feelings. Valence is a result of whatever biology programs into us as well as the results of early experience. These influence the roles that we are most likely to be scripted into—but they are not the totality of who we "are." Our distress in relationships is often that we are repeatedly chosen to play parts that we may no longer wish to enact. This was Mark's dilemma. He wanted to claim the feeling side of himself but was too locked into being "the rational man" for all those who mattered most to him and counted on his rationality.

Like actors who find themselves invited only to play the villain or the hero, ordinary people may be continually enlisted to enact certain parts for others. And like the "tough guy" actor who wants to play a more complex role—or Mark who wanted to express something else in himself—people may find it difficult to persuade the important people in their lives to allow them to transform their way of being. Very often, people who wish to change find themselves up against the dictates of others' scripts, which seem to insist that they either perform their accustomed role or leave the stage. While we are main characters in our own dramas, we are subordinate players in the dramas of others, and each drama bounds and limits the others (MacIntyre, 1981). Like great actors (and actresses), most people have a wide repertory of roles they can enact—if only given the right circumstances to do so.

Being aware of these processes doesn't necessarily tell us how to change the roles we are enacting, but it may help us better understand our interpersonal life and maintain a clearer awareness of our own subjectivity. I recall a conversation I had with one of my mentors, Margaret Rioch, who taught me (or enabled me to learn) much of what I now understand about the processes I have tried to describe here. She was, at the time of this conversation, in her late seventies, a much revered, venerated guru among us, a group of midcareer psychologists who were studying with her. But I also knew her well enough to know that she, like us, struggled with all she didn't know or understand (even though we didn't like to think that there was anything she didn't know or understand). "With all you've taught us about the irrationality of idealization," I asked her, "how can you bear us placing you in the role of such a goddess?" With her customary great wisdom, she replied simply, "Someone has to do it." What I learned from this is that we can accept others' idealizations, even enact them, but we don't have to confuse this with who we "are."

INDIVIDUALISM AND RELATIONAL CULTURES

In our individualistic culture, we construct and value a bounded self that is, in its most esteemed form, fully "independent" of others. By doing so, we blind ourselves to the fundamentally intersubjective nature of ourselves as people. Our emotional lives are lived in tandem as we unconsciously, but continually, pass feelings from one to another. What we cannot bear to feel we deposit in another, thereby creating the other as a repository for what we disown in ourselves. These processes are inevitable but, because they are unconscious, very difficult to notice in operation. They are also highly complex, such that the metaphor of the individual becomes a convenient way to speak about interpersonal reality.

Individualism is a comforting intellectual conceit because it simplifies interpersonal reality and tends to focus on behavior or reportable internal states. Mutual interpersonal creation, however, is affective—felt rather than seen. As infant studies are showing, we sense the other person's internal and emotional state and the mutuality (or lack of mutuality) in their fit with us long before we have language for it.[8]

Our society determines how we interpret our felt experience of others by bequeathing to us a language that categorizes others' ways of being with us. In Western society, this language consists largely of individualistic, essentialist trait terms. Language determines what we can and cannot express or even perceive. Moreover, we have few words to express the mutuality of interpersonal exchange. Thus, we can say Georgia is "kind," but we do not say Georgia and I have constructed an interpersonal reality in which I evoke her kindness and she evokes my gratitude or my reciprocal kindness or my resentment and envy, etc. Leadership is a property of the followers, but our language constructs leadership as residing in an individual. We can only teach those who think they have something to learn from us, yet we treat the term *teacher* as independent of the students who create the possibility of learning.

In Japanese culture, one honors another by inviting them to indulge you in some way—this is the concept of *amae*. In the United States, one is indebted to the one who indulges you—this is the concept of "I owe you." Through language, we together construct the relational world that we live in—a language that carries the stories that instruct us in how to interpret how we are with one another.

The linguistically favored categories of what we notice among others organizes a (sub)culture of experience that bounds our forms of relationship to one another. In past centuries in our own culture, people were responded to and judged in terms of whether or not they were "God-fearing," a stamp of social approval. Today, this term is no longer part of the larger Western discourse, and one is quite unlikely to classify people in this way except in certain isolated religious communities. However, every subgroup of people has its favored terms for how people are viewed, and this goes beyond approving or disapproving of them. There is an emotional language that constructs the culture of relationships through defining what aspects of relational life are attended to.

It is fundamentally human to need connection to others—connection for security, attachment, validation, mutuality, and sexual satisfaction (Josselson, 1992). We also need others to model for us ways of being and to connect us to a wider sense of belonging in a community. And we need others to care for so that we feel that what we have to give is worthwhile. Fulfillment of these needs is patterned differently for every person, and culture prescribes how we interpret the behaviors that may or may not satisfy these relational needs.

Before the feminist movement, for example, a "good husband" was defined as one who makes a good living, is faithful, does not drink to excess, or physically assault his wife. But then "sensitivity" and "responsiveness" became prized in potential husbands, much to the consternation and confusion of many men who, understandably, felt that expectations of them had radically shifted. Many men had few experiences to be able to determine whether they were "sensitive" or not—and the processes of learning about this became the source of much of the humor of the 1970s and 1980s. This was simply not a relational category that had meaning to many men. Those who were able, then, had to find ways to be inducted into the growing culture of "sensitivity."

Advertising agencies are well aware of the semiotics of relationship, as they construct advertisements for diamonds, flowers, lingerie, and many other things implying that the bestowal of such gifts (from a man to a woman) is an avowal of romantic passion—or enduring love. The culture continues to argue over whether one can be a "good enough mother" and leave a child in daycare. I am still trying to understand what it means to have dozens of "friends" on Friendster.com.

Culture is a set of social agreements on how to see the world (Myerhoff, 1978). Relational culture is constructed by language and events that highlight certain aspects of interaction, foregrounding them and making them salient. The (sub)culture in which we grow and live allows us a range of ways to construct others as it dictates, through language, what we may perceive in others. A relationship is always a dialogue between two personal universes (Stolorow and Atwood, 1992) that defines what is to be noticed.

Among the life histories we have considered, we can observe how relational structures are used to construct widely varying "cultures" of experience. For Donna and Roberta, their culture is one of playing "hot potato" with dependency, their twinship making them highly sensitive to issues of merger and separateness, a theme which then colors all their other relationships. Donna and Roberta, both highly expressive of their feelings, would, I imagine, be mystified and chagrined by the relational culture of Mark and Joan, who live in a culture of obligation, with a firm barrier erected between duty and feeling. Theirs is a world of stylized interactions where people do what is expected of them but suppress their emotional reactions. As they describe their relational worlds and the people who have mattered to them over their lives, they attend to who has and has not made it possible for them to express the walled-off emotional realities that each has been at pains to find a place for in their lives. Feeling so bounded in their private worlds, struggling to make meaningful emotional contact with others, the sensitivity of Donna and Roberta to issues of merger and separateness would make little sense. It would be as though they were speaking a different language. In contrasting these pairs, the linguistic/emotional disparity between their relational cultures is apparent.

Lavinia has constructed a world in which nurturing is the primary currency of exchange, while her mother Mary's world revolved around being special to men, thus putting her outside Lavinia's reach, no matter how tenderly Lavinia cared for her. For Lavinia, though, people exist to be taken care of and life becomes a process of managing resentment about being in this caretaker role and finding others for "support." Nurturing and supporting form the axis of the relational culture in which she—and the others she has recruited in her drama—live. Tom and Kathy created their relationship when each most needed "security," and "being there" for one another was the basis of their relational culture. But Kathy moved into an unfamiliar culture of relationships that required new definitions and Tom was left enacting security with no one to secure. Within his relational world of duty and loyalty where he could predictably fulfill the roles he had taken on (and assumed that others would do so as well), Tom had to find a way to make sense of a betrayal that had no meaning in his world. Kathy, who started out to study psychology for its intellectual challenges, found herself thrust, through her new friends and teachers, into a world of inner exploration that opened for her previously unimagined vistas of relational experience and made her earlier pact of reliability and safety no longer fulfilling. Together, then, people create relational worlds that privilege certain aspects of interpersonal life—and these are negotiated worlds, not ones the individual determines alone. Dynamic systems involve the cooperative interaction of their elements and cannot be predicted by observing just one individual.

We live within the framework of a legal code that constructs the individual as an autonomous agent with free will (with a few exceptions). Morally, the individual is taken to be responsible for his or her own actions. To adult ears, the "s/he made me do it" defense sounds childish, silly, or reprehensible. Yet, if we fully understand the complexity of the interconnection of selves, others are indeed implicated in our actions, as we are implicated in theirs. This is marvelously portrayed in the movie *In the Bedroom*, in which a respectable couple, bereaved after the murder of their college-aged son, attempts to cope with their grief and rage. The husband, Matt, mild-mannered, calm, laid back, seems to be intensely experiencing the sense of loss while his wife, Ruth, is nearly paralyzed with rage. Suffering their anguish privately and alone, Matt and Ruth say little to one another until eventually Ruth explodes at Matt and accuses him of having vicariously enjoyed their son's affair, which led to his murder. Emptied temporarily of her rage, she collapses in pain and tells Matt how excruciating it is for her to run into their son's murderer, free on bail, on the streets of their small town. Shortly after this intense conversation, Matt kills the murderer in a cold, calculated scene. And we, the viewers, are left to wonder if this killing is on behalf of his own rage—or Ruth's. He fired the gun; she powered the act, even though they never discussed it. She had been experiencing the rage for both of them until he expressed it. Legally, of course, he "committed" the killing. But psychologically, the story is much more layered and complex. In the final scene, she is satisfied and relieved and seems to know what he did without his having to tell her. And, for the viewer, it is the hovering presence of an act conceived between people, out of the intensity of their shared grief and rage, that makes the film so haunting.

The boundary between self and other is much more porous than our theories depict. How we construct one another and take one another to be part of ourselves becomes part of the fabric of what we think, feel, believe, are, and do. The formulation of the concept of "co-dependency" was an effort to bring into awareness one aspect of these phenomena. The idea that one can "enable" someone else to behave in self-destructive ways helped to clarify the ways in which one person can unwittingly be involved in another's actions.

Why do we take part in others' dramas—even when we recognize that we are acting in a script that does not suit us? We do so because of the deep, unconscious, and terribly painful fear that if we are not enacting what others need, we will cease to exist for them at all. The most terrible fear is not of being harmed, but of being annihilated—of simply disappearing as meaningful in the lives of those we love. In order to avoid this, people will go to great lengths and bear all manner of torment. For the person in an abusive relationship, it is better to endure abuse than not to exist at all. Thus, we willingly, perhaps even eagerly, accept our role assignments; being on someone's stage is better than being alone in the cold and dark outside. For every person, the sense of significance in life is a feeling of place in other people's worlds. We will each go to great lengths to feel that we have meaning for others and we will sometimes have to settle for enacting a role that we might not have (consciously) wished for. As we look back on our lives, our autobiographies are no more or less than the sum of who we have been for others and who they have been for us. And, of course, there are many people whose life script is always to be miscast or undercast—this, too, is a kind of drama.

Thinking in relational terms, then, involves a radical shift in attention. The "individual," in this view, becomes a product of a relational network that finds and creates, is found by and created by, the others in the system, in an endless flow of mutual interaction.

RELATIONAL PATTERNING

Another way of simplifying the complexity of the intersubjective world
has been to focus on the dyad. This has been the strategy of both relational
researchers and therapists as they ask about people's relationships with
their mothers or fathers or spouses.[9] But, as we have seen, the availability
of roles depends on the other characters on the director's stage and to understand the relational universe of the individual, we have to be mindful
of the whole cast. For both Mary and Lavinia, aunts played crucial roles
in providing the nurturing and empathy they could not find in their
mothers. Mary was able to maintain herself in her marriage because she
found Kevin to value her outside the boundaries of her marriage. Donna
"found" herself through her relationship with her mentor and friend
while keeping Roberta available for her (disavowed) more childlike
needs. Kathy was able to reconstruct her experience of her relationship to
Tom through the engaged help of her friends who brought a new vocabulary and viewpoint that enabled her to leave him.

A person appears to be different in each relationship because the
"other" he or she has created expresses different aspects of the internal
world. The "saintly" person (here Gandhi is a good example) can exemplify moral kindness in their public activities while being self-centered
and demeaning to those at home. If we can begin to think in terms of the
repertory of roles, within the individual and among others, we get a truer
picture of relational life than if we think of people "being" the part they
play in a single relationship.

When we look across a life retrospectively, we also find that the meanings of others evolve, transform, or fade. Relationships that have intense
emotional significance at one period of life may be nearly devoid of meaning later on. In some cases, others have been in some way absorbed into
the self or the play has changed and the role is no longer in demand—or,
as often happens in enduring relationships, the players learn to take mod-
ified parts in each other's scripts. While psychology and psychoanalysis
have understood a good deal about the shaping effects of early relationships, what lasting impact later relationships have on a life, how they assume autobiographical importance, is still relatively unexplored.

BEYOND ILLUSION

To meet another person without preconception, with no script to place
them in, is perhaps an ideal but not a possibility. Bion (1967) proposed the
idea of meeting the other "without memory or desire" and then trying to
observe the aspects of oneself called forth by the other in the present mo-

ment. Psychoanalysts have been striving to be "blank slates" for years but always falling short—and then reflecting on their failure to do so as a way of trying to get nearer to the ideal. What resonates in us in response to the other is always a product of our past relationships and our preconceptions. We cannot understand anything new without first assimilating it to what has gone before. This, as the philosopher Heidegger pointed out, is our horizon of understanding, the only standpoint from which we are able to think at all. As we meet a person, he or she may remind us, even unconsciously, of an old relationship, but as the relationship develops and if we allow ourselves to encounter surprise, the experience then enlarges our categories and understandings of others. The next new person is then taken in against a wider repertoire of possibility. But it is important to keep in mind that this is taking place on both sides. At the same time that I am responding to you in terms of my previous emotional knowledge of people and relationships, you are responding to me in terms of yours, which of course, shapes the way in which I view you, and my responsiveness shapes how you view me. As R. D. Laing (1967) pointed out, this gets even more complicated in that each person (A) also has a reading of how the other (B) is thinking about them and how A is thinking about what B is thinking about what A is thinking about B. In a bit plainer language, "I can't stand it that you think that I think that you think I am a failure." Written this way, it seems abstruse and hard to follow, but this is what people are doing all the time as they monitor each other's reaction to them and create scenarios about what the other is thinking and feeling.

The difficulty, even tragedy, of human life is that the others who form our world are always more (or less) than our construction of them. Thus, misunderstandings are inevitable. In one of Shakespeare's greatest tragedies, King Lear asks for words of love from his daughters before he parcels his kingdom out to them. His youngest daughter, Cordelia, the one who truly loves him, is so certain that he knows of the authenticity of her love that she refuses to speak ("my love's/ More richer than my tongue"). For her, her love is apparent to her father and words could not contain it, indeed would only tarnish it. In her mind, she is differentiating herself from what she knows to be the artifice of her greedy sisters' self-serving and inauthentic proclamations of love. Lear, however, constructs love to be obedience and he regards Cordelia's failure to speak as insolent pride, not love. Thus, through misconstruing her (and she misconstruing him), he engenders his own ruin.

TOWARD MORE KNOWLEDGE OF THE OTHER

With too much distance, we regard others through the projections of stereotypes. But with too much proximity, there are different but no less important distortions. The closer we are to someone, the less clearly we can see him or her. Intimacy muddies our vision and engulfs the other with our own internal realities. The optimal distance from which we can see and hear the other clearly in his or her own terms is rarely achieved.

We are most cognizant of our own processes of illusion when we become aware of a different view of the same person. There are moments when someone we love seems, perhaps just for a brief instant, like a stranger and we see her or him with different eyes. Or, if we see perhaps a former lover, after a long period of time, we may wonder, "What did I ever see in him/her?" These counterviews of another person make us aware of the ways in which our constructions endow others with meaning.

There is a wide gulf between knowledge and belief, and we are apt to confuse the two when it comes to our relations with others. Knowledge refers to certainty about external reality, while belief acknowledges our own role in constructing a picture of what exists outside of ourselves.[10] We think we "know" a person, but it takes only a few bits of knowledge for us to create a character who internally represents this person and to whom we then respond, and from the time we decide we "know" someone, we begin responding more to our own invention than to the reality of the other person. When people are actors in our private theater, we attend only to what is meaningful in the script, theirs and ours, but this always involves omitting other aspects of who they (and we) are. We know our own complexity better than we can hope to know another's; we recognize the multiplicity of our own emotional experience, the ways in which we experience many feelings at the same time—or shifting feelings at different times. Yet we tend to represent others as finite in dimension— not necessarily one-dimensional, because this would be too simple, but limited in dimensions, as "fixed" or secured rather than in flux. We can attune to some, but not all, of another's internal experience. Empathic knowing of another's subjectivity is an extremely difficult, and often exhausting, task.[11] Really listening to another person is one of the most arduous challenges we ever undertake, for it means encountering the strange world that the other inhabits—a world alien from our own (Levinas, 1999). At the same time, we crave to be known by others for we can only feel ourselves to be a self if someone else recognizes us as who we experience ourselves to be (Benjamin, 1988).

The philosopher Martin Buber (1965, 1970) distinguished between "I-it" relationships in which the other is made use of for our own purposes and "I-thou" relationships in which there is true meeting between souls. These latter, he concluded, are rare in life. I would agree that true "I-thou" relating is rare, but I think that we do not create "I-it" relationships out of any nefarious purpose. We imagine others to be what we think they are and then find it hard to question our own invention, an invention that seems to us like an unchangeable given of reality.

Without illusion, there would be no relationship. Generally, this works out well enough as we create with family members, friends, and partners interlocking dramas that are reasonably satisfying to all the players. Mutual creations and discoveries are interacting harmoniously as we enact the unconsciously agreed upon roles in one another's scripts. When relationships are going well, our illusions are sustainable and we can sidestep Winnicott's terror-inducing question of whether I found you or created you: You tell a joke, I laugh; I succeed, you applaud; I need solace, you comfort; you are scatterbrained, I organize things; I need to feel powerful, you need to be led—together we create a whole. We can agree that we "love" each other without having to inquire too deeply into what love means to each of us.

People are bonded through their mutual creations, each carrying a part of the other that the other either can't recognize (in terms of positive aspects) or can't bear (negative ones) in the self.[12] If everyone is satisfied with the arrangement of parts, they will feel comfortably connected. Interpersonal harmony, in this view, is not the absence of illusion or projective identifications—it is the complementarity of them. But, as we have seen, we can also enlist people to be villains and spend our lives defending ourselves against them, we can create people as needy and spend our lives enslaved to them or, as parents, create children as disowned parts of ourselves and then punish or reject them for it (or hope they will redeem us).

Trying to recognize our projections means acknowledging to ourselves that how we see people is not the totality of how they "are" and thereby becoming open to new knowledge of them. The process of psychotherapy generally involves recognizing aspects of important people in one's life that were overshadowed by other representations of them. The person with the "perfect" mother has to come to terms with the ways in which mother was also disappointing; the person with the rejecting mother learns to realize emotionally the ways in which she was also loving. Villains can also be kind. And the most generous people also have their spiteful sides. The nature of relationships is always ambivalent—filled with love and hate. It is the effort to keep these powerful feelings apart that leads to the distortions. The more we really "know" people, the more complex they will appear and the more contradictory will be our feelings toward them.

Indeed, nearly forty years of experience as a therapist has taught me that what most changes in an intensive therapy is one's experience of self with others as one learns more and more about how one's own individual ways of creating others circumscribe and limit the kinds of relationships with others that one can have. The more we need someone to be a certain way, the less we can acknowledge him or her as an independent subject. When we have sculpted people out of our own need, our relationship with them becomes fulfilling—but lifeless. Only when Galatea came to life and had an existence independent of him could Pygmalion have a vital relationship with her—but we are left to imagine the discoveries he might have had to make about her. After only a short time of lived experience, she would have become more than what he had sculpted her to be. Can we envision Pygmalion trying to "discover" her from her own vibrant center—which would, of course, include what she may need him to be for her?[13]

Processes of illusion and of creating the other through projective identification are experienced as certainty about the other. Like Galatea in the Pygmalion myth, the other is cast in stone and finalized by our perceptions. Such relationships are self-perpetuating and repetitive since nothing new is allowed to blossom. In order to foster vitality in our relationships, we must add to our inevitable illusions a fuller awareness of aspects of the other person's inner experience. If we relate to others from a stance of curiosity, of *not* knowing who they are and how they feel, we are alert to their subjectivity. We allow ourselves to be surprised. If we want to better understand our relationships, we have to ask, "What is your experience of yourself?"—and the even more difficult "What is your experience of me?" Then we have to be prepared, without defensiveness, to hear the answers. This is difficult, however, because we have a stake in being seen a certain way by those we love (our attachment to the aspect of them we have created) and to be conjured otherwise is to risk feeling insulted or demeaned. We are unlikely to hear only what we wish to hear, which is why such explorations are usually reserved for contained encounters such as psychotherapy, group therapy, or group relations and personal growth conferences.[14]

Sometimes people can find their own way to becoming an audience to their own scenarios, observing what is being portrayed and discovering means of reworking the script. Relational dialogue has built-in uncertainty, moments of unpredictability where the roles could change and something new can emerge, but this takes conscious effort and reflection—or at least, some impetus to overcome the automaticity of relational scripts.[15]

Who other people are, of course, will include their own illusions (projections)—but rather than telling them that what they experience isn't so when it doesn't match our perceptions, we must try to understand that this is the reality from within which they live—just as who *we* are includes our own illusions. There is no "correct" version of interpersonal reality— only the intersection of personal universes. But as we are invested in our own sense of reality, our tendency is to try to make our own experience dominate or annihilate the other. Only through trying to understand one another as independent but mutually constructed centers of experience can we achieve the "meeting" that Buber described.

When there is strife from a mismatch of scripts, we require a space for reflection where we can wonder about what role we may have had in creating that which we find intolerable in the other person. Can we take back as part of ourselves something we may have asked the other to carry for us? Can we give back something we are carrying for them? Similarly, when someone is filled with deference (or envy) to those who are so much more admirable, we wonder about whether the person can take back the idealization, stop trying to live through the other, and reclaim his or her own talents.

The more we are able to own all of our own parts, even the ones we find hard to bear in ourselves, the less we need to enlist others to carry these parts for us. The alert therapist, rather than joining the patient to cement a construction of the other, asks where that element lies in the patient. With the patient who says, My husband constantly ignores and rejects me, the therapist wonders, And how do you ignore and reject him? There is no point in asking this since the patient will not know (and would feel accused and assaulted by the question), but it is still an important question to ponder. Aggression and distance are in the system and both parties are enacting it. Too often the therapeutically blessed solution has been for the patient to disengage herself or leave the relationship—with no recognition of the unconscious dialogue and shared participation that creates the interaction.

Patients come to therapy when they find themselves locked into scripts that are stultifying to them or when their own scripts are failing. Psychodynamically oriented therapists, working in long-term intensive therapy, will await being recruited into the unpalatable scripts and then use their own experience with the patients to try to free them. But therapists from other orientations as well can use their understanding of these processes by which interpersonal reality is constructed to assist their patients in reassessing the meanings they have made of their relationship. Across therapeutic schools and belief systems, we can join in recognition that there is always more of the Other to know.

NOTES

1. Kathy consulted me for psychotherapy twelve years after the initial meeting I had with her following her separation from Tom.

2. We can only reflect on relationships in terms that are already present in our interior world. Schutz (1967) argues that experiences are meaningful only when

they are grasped reflectively. The meaning is the *way* in which the ego regards its experience.

3. Laing (1969), p. 87.

4. www.script-o-rama.com/movie_scripts/s/some-like-it-hot-script.html.

5. Research on mother-infant interaction has led to reconceptualization of the psychoanalytic situation in intersubjective terms and efforts to detail relational exchanges at a moment-to-moment level to witness the co-creation of the relationship. See especially, Lyons-Ruth (1999), The Boston Change Process Study Group (1998 and 2002), and Beebe and Lachman (2002).

6. Social psychologists have demonstrated, using questionnaire measures, that dating college student couples who idealized one another had more durable relationships and actually created the relationships they wished for as romances progressed (Murray, Holmes, and Griffin, 1996) and that affirming behavior from a close partner can help the self move toward its ideal self (Rusbult et al., 2005). Rosenthal (2002) coined the term "Pygmalion effect" in the 1960s to refer to the phenomena that students perform better when their teachers are led to believe that they have untapped intellectual potential. Later termed expectancy effects or the self-fulfilling prophecy, it has also been demonstrated in work settings that positive beliefs about others enhance their performance—but there are arguments among researchers about the exact conditions necessary for these inductions to produce results.

7. Ferenczi (1917) referred to this process as a dialogue of the unconscious.

8. See Tronick (1989), Weinberg and Tronick (1994), and Trevarthen (1993).

9. I am aware that, in this book, I have also highlighted dyads—not because I think that dyads are central, but because larger systems get overly complex to analyze closely in written language. Certainly, it would add to our understanding to have considered relational patternings and interpretive narratives from the other players in the lives of the main characters of chapters 3–6.

10. See Britton (1995) and Target and Fonagy (1996).

11. Jessica Benjamin (2004) and Thomas Ogden (1994) have been developing the concept of "thirdness" in which it becomes possible to recognize the other's point of view without surrendering one's own.

12. See Dicks (1963), Scharff and Scharff (1991), and Sander (2004) for how this applies to married couples. Because the nature of the bond is different for each couple, it becomes difficult for marriage researchers to locate universal predictors of happy or stable marriages. See Bradbury (1998).

13. Shaw was not a romantic in this regard. He ends his sequel to the play by saying, "Galatea never does quite like Pygmalion: his relation to her is too godlike to be altogether agreeable."

14. In Irvin Yalom's (1995, 2002) view, interpersonal learning, discovering (and changing) who one is for others and who others are to the self, is the heart of psychotherapy.

15. Some psychoanalysts argue that change in implicit relational experience can occur through enactments of new forms without cognitive mediation or symbolization in language (Boston Change Process Study Group, 2002 and Lyons-Ruth, 1999).

References

Acitelli, L. K., and Holmberg, D. 1993. Reflecting on relationships: The role of thoughts and memories. *Advances in Personal Relationships*, 4, 71–100.

Apter, T., and Josselson, R. 1998. *Best friends: The pleasures and perils of girls' and women's friendships*. New York: Crown.

Aron, L. 1996. *A meeting of minds*. Hillsdale, NJ: Analytic Press.

Bargh, J. A., and Chartrand, T. L. 1999. The unbearable automaticity of being. *American Psychologist*, 54, 462–79.

Beebe, B., and Lachmann, F. M. 1988. The contribution of mother-infant mutual influence to the origins of self and object representations. *Psychoanalytic Psychology*, 5, 305–37.

———. 1998. Co-constructing inner and relational processes: Self- and mutual regulation in infant research and adult treatment. *Psychoanalytic Psychology*, 15(4), 480–516.

———. 2002. *Infant research and adult treatment: Coconstructing interactions*. Hillsdale, NJ: Analytic Press.

Beebe, B., Lachmann, F. M., and Jaffe, J. 1997. Mother-infant interaction structures and presymbolic self- and object representations. *Psychoanalytic Dialogues*, 7, 133–82.

Benjamin, J. 1988. *The bonds of love*. New York: Pantheon.

———. 2004. Beyond doer and done to: An intersubjective view of thirdness. *Psychoanalytic Quarterly*, 73(1), 5–46.

Bion, W. R. 1959. *Experiences in groups*. New York: Basic Books.

———. 1962. *Learning from experience*. London: W. Heinemann.

———. 1967. Notes on memory and desire. *Psychoanalytic Forum*, 2, 271–86.

Bollas, C. 1987. *The shadow of the object: Psychoanalysis of the unthought known*. New York: Columbia University Press.

Boston Change Process Study Group (Stern, D. N., Sander, L. W., Nahum, J. P., Harrison, A. M., Lyons-Ruth, K., Morgan, A. C., Bruschweilerstern, N., and

Tronick, E. Z). 1998. Report 1. Non-interpretive mechanisms in psychoanalytic therapy: The something more than interpretation. *International Journal of Psychoanalysis*, 79, 908–21.

———. 2002. Explicating the implicit: The local level and microprocess of change in the analytic situation. *International Journal of Psychoanalysis*, 83, 1051–62.

———. n.d. The "something more" than interpretation revisited: Sloppiness and co-creativity in the psychoanalytic encounter. http://www.psybc.com/pdfs/library/SomethingMorecommentaries.pdf

Bradbury, T., ed. 1998. *The developmental course of marital dysfunction.* New York: Cambridge University Press.

Britton, R. 1995. Psychic reality and unconscious belief. *International Journal of Psychoanalysis*, 76, 19–23.

Brunet, L., and Casoni, D. 1996. A review of the concepts of symbolization and projective identification in regards to the patient's use of the analyst. *Canadian Journal of Psychoanalysis*, 4, 109–27.

Buber, M. 1965. *The knowledge of man.* New York: HarperCollins.

———. 1970. *I and thou.* New York: Scribners.

Catherall, D. R. 1992. Working with projective identification in couples. *Family Process*, 31, 355–67.

Cimino, C., and Correale, A. 2005. Projective identification and consciousness alteration: A bridge between psychoanalysis and neuroscience? *International Journal of Psychoanalysis*, 86, 1, 51–60.

Dicks, H. 1963. Object relations and marital studies. *British Journal of Medical Psychology*, 36, 125–29.

———. 1967. *Marital tensions.* New York: Basic Books.

Eakin, P. 1999. *How our lives become stories.* Ithaca: Cornell University Press.

Emde, R. N. 1983. The prerepresentational self and its affective core. *Psychoanal. Study Child* 38, 165–92.

Ferenczi, S. 1917. Letter from Sándor Ferenczi to Sigmund Freud, December 25, 1917. *The correspondence of Sigmund Freud and Sándor Ferenczi,* volume 2, 1914–1919, 254–56.

Freud, S. 1915. *The unconscious.* Trans. J. Strachey. In Standard Edition, 14 (pp. 166–215). London: Hogarth Press, 1957.

Gadamer, H. 1979. *Philosophical hermeneutics.* Trans. D. E. Linge. Berkeley: University of California Press.

Gergen, K. J. 1994. *Realities and relationships: Soundings in social construction.* Cambridge, MA: Harvard University Press.

———. 1999. *An invitation to social construction.* London: Sage.

Gillette, J., and McCollom, M., eds. 1995. *Groups in context: A new perspective on group dynamics.* Lanham, MD: University Press of America.

Goffman, E. 1961. *Encounters: Two studies in the sociology of interaction.* Indianapolis: Bobbs-Merrill.

Gordon. M. 1996. *The shadow man: A daughter's search for her father.* New York: Random House.

Greatrex, T. S. 2002. Projective identification. *Journal of Neuro-psychoanalysis*, 4, 187–97.

Grotstein, J. S. 1981. *Splitting and projective identification.* New York: Jason Aronson.

Hirschhorn, L. 1988. *The workplace within*. Cambridge, MA: MIT Press.

Joseph, B. 1987. Projective identification: Clinical aspects. In J. Sandler (ed.), *Projection, identification, projective identification* (pp. 65–76). Madison, CT: Int. Univ. Press.

Josselson, R. 1992. *The space between us: Exploring the dimensions of human relationships*. San Francisco: Jossey-Bass.

Kahneman, D. 2003. A perspective on judgment and choice: Mapping bounded rationality. *American Psychologist*, 58 (9), 697–720.

Knight, R. 1940. Introjection, projection and identification. *Psychoanal. Quarterly*, 9, 334–41.

Laing, R. D. 1967. *The politics of experience*. New York: Ballantine Books.

———. 1969. *Self and others*. London: Tavistock Publications.

Lear, J. 2002. Jumping from the couch. *International Journal of Psychoanalysis*, 83, 583–95.

Lerner, H. G. 1985. *The dance of anger*. New York: Harper and Row.

———. 1989. *The dance of intimacy*. New York: Harper and Row.

Levinas, E. 1999. *Alterity and transcendence*. New York: Columbia University Press.

Lotz, M. 1991. Projective identification on different levels. *Scandinavian Psychoanal. Review*, 14, 19–38.

Lyons-Ruth, K. 1999. The two-person unconscious: Intersubjective dialogue, enactive relational representation, and the emergence of new forms of relational organization. *Psychoanal. Inquiry, 19*, 576–617.

MacIntyre, A. 1981. *After virtue*. Notre Dame, IN: University of Notre Dame Press.

Malin, A. 1966. Projective identification in the therapeutic process. *International Journal of Psychoanalysis*, 47, 26–31.

McDougall, J. 1985. *Theaters of the mind*. New York: Basic Books.

Middelberg, C. 2001. Projective identification in common couples dances. *Journal of Marital and Family Therapy*, 27, 3, 341–53.

Mikulincer, M., and Horesh, N. 1999. Adult attachment style and the perception of others: The role of projective mechanisms. *Journal of Personality and Social Psychology*, 76, 1022–34.

Mitchell, S. A. 1988. *Relational concepts in psychoanalysis* Cambridge, MA: Harvard University Press.

———. 1999. Attachment theory and the psychoanalytic tradition. *Psychoanalytic Dialogues*, 9, 85–107.

Murray, S. L., and Holmes, J. G. 1992. Seeing virtues in faults: Negativity and the transformation of interpersonal narratives in close relationships. *Journal of Personality and Social Psychology*, 65, 4, 707–22.

Murray, S. L., Holmes, J. G., Bellavia, G., Griffin, D. W., and Dolderman, D. 2002. Kindred spirits? The benefits of egocentrism in close relationships. *Journal of Personality and Social Psychology*, 82, 563–81.

Murray, S. L., Holmes, J. G., and Griffin, D. W. 1996. The self-fulfilling nature of positive illusions in romantic relationships: Love is not blind, but prescient. *Journal of Personality and Social Psychology*, 71, 6, 1155–80.

Myerhoff, B. 1979. *Number our days*. New York: Dutton.

Ogden, T. H. 1979. On projective identification. *International Journal of Psychoanalysis*, 60, 357–73.

——. 1982. *Projective identification and psychotherapeutic technique.* New York: Jason Aronson.

——. 1992. The dialectically constituted/decentred subject of psychoanalysis II. The contributions of Klein and Winnicott. *International Journal of Psychoanalysis,* 73, 613–26.

——. 1994. The analytic third: Working with intersubjective clinical facts. *International Journal of Psychoanalysis,* 75, 3–20.

Rice, A. K. 1965. *Learning for leadership: Interpersonal and intergroup relations.* London: Tavistock Publications.

Ricoeur, P. 1992. *Oneself as another.* Trans. K. Blaney. Chicago: University of Chicago Press.

Rosenthal, R. 2002. Covert communications in classrooms, clinics, courtrooms, and cubicles. *American Psychologist,* 57, 839–49.

Ross, M., and Holmberg, D. 1992. Are wives' memories for events in relationships more vivid than their husbands' memories? *Journal of Social and Personal Relationships,* 9, 585–604.

Rusbult, C. E., Kumashiro, M., Stocker, S. L., Kirchner, J. L., Fnkel, E. J., and Coolsen, M. K. 2005. Self processes in interdependent relationships: Partner affirmation and the Michelangelo phenomenon. *Interaction Studies,* 6, 3, 375–91.

Rychlak, J. F. 1988. *The psychology of rigorous humanism.* 2nd ed. New York: New York University Press.

Sander, F. M. 2004. Psychoanalytic couple therapy: Classical style. *Psychoanalytic Inquiry,* 24, 3, 373–86.

Sandler, J. 1990. On internal object relations. *Journal of the American Psychoanal. Association,* 38, 859–79.

——. ed. 1987. *Projection, identification, projective identification.* Madison, CT: Int. Univ. Press.

Scharff, D. E., and Scharff, J. S. 1991. *Object relations couple therapy.* Northvale, NJ: Jason Aronson.

Schore, A. N. 1994. *Affect regulation and the origin of the self.* Hillsdale, NJ: Lawrence Erlbaum.

——. 2001. The right brain as the neurobiological substratum of Freud's dynamic unconscious. In D. E. Scharff (ed.), *The psychoanalytic century* (pp. 61–88). New York: Other Press.

Schutz, A. 1967. *Phenomenology of the social world.* Trans. G. Walsh and F. Lehnert. Evanston, IL: Northwestern University Press.

Segal, H. 1964. *Introduction to the work of Melanie Klein.* London: Heinemann; New York: Basic Books.

Seligman, S. 1999. Integrating Kleinian theory and intersubjective infant research. *Psychoanal. Dialogues,* 9, 129–59.

Shapiro, E., and Carr, A. 1991. *Lost in familiar places: Creating new connections between the individual and society.* New Haven, CT: Yale University Press.

Steedman, C. K. 1986. *Landscape for a good woman: A story of two lives.* New York: Rutgers University Press.

Stolorow, R. D., and Atwood, G. E. 1992. *Contexts of being.* Hillsdale, NJ: Analytic Press.

Stolorow, R. D., Orange, D., and Atwood, G. E. 2001. Cartesian and post-Cartesian trends in relational psychoanalysis. *Psychoanalytic Psychology,* 18, 3, 468–84.

Target, M., and Fonagy, P. 1996. Playing with reality: II. The development of psychic reality from a theoretical perspective. *International Journal of Psychoanalysis,* 77, 459–79.

Tolstoy. L. *War and peace.* Trans. Constance Garnett. New York: Carleton House.

Trevarthen, C. 1993. The function of emotions in early infant communication and development. In J. Nadel and L. Camaioni (eds.), *New perspectives in early communicative development* (pp. 48–81). London: Routledge.

Tronick, E. 1989. Emotions and emotional communication in infants. *American Psychologist,* 44, 112–19.

Valle, R. S., and King, M. 1978. *Existential-phenomenological alternatives for psychology.* New York: Oxford University Press.

Volkan, V. D. 1997. *Bloodlines: From ethnic pride to ethnic terrorism.* New York: Farrar, Straus and Giroux.

———. 2004. *Blind trust: Large groups and their leaders in times of crises and terror.* Charlottesville, VA: Pitchstone Publishing.

Weinberg, M. K., and Tronick, E. Z. 1994. Beyond the face: An empirical study of infant affective configurations of facial, vocal, gestural, and regulatory behaviors. *Child Development,* 65, 1503–15.

Willi, J. 1984. The concept of collusion: A theoretical framework for martial therapy. *Family Process,* 23, 177–86.

Winnicott, D. W. 1975 [1951]. Transitional objects and transitional phenomena. In D. W. Winnicott, *Through paediatrics to psychoanalysis.* London: Hogarth Press.

Yalom, I. 1995. *The theory and practice of group psychotherapy.* 4th ed. New York: Basic Books.

———. 2002. *The gift of therapy.* New York: HarperCollins.

Young-Bruehl, E. 1996. *The anatomy of prejudices.* Cambridge, MA: Harvard University Press.

Index

About the Author

Ruthellen Josselson, Ph.D., ABPP, is a professor of psychology at the Fielding Graduate University and was formerly a professor at the Hebrew University of Jerusalem and at Harvard University. Recipient of the Henry A. Murray Award from the American Psychological Association and a Fulbright Fellowship, she is also a practicing psychotherapist. Her research interests focus on the use of narrative to understand people's life histories and she has authored several books on relationships (among them: *The Space Between Us: Exploring the Dimensions of Human Relationships* and, with Terri Apter, *Best Friends: The Pleasures and Perils of Girls' and Women's Friendships.*) Her other books focus on women's identity, including *Revising Herself: The Story of Women's Identity from College to Midlife*, which received the Delta Kappa Gamma International Educators' Award. She has also co-edited the series *The Narrative Study of Lives*.